W9-AKV-625

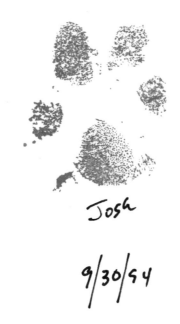

Josh

9/30/94

JOSH
The Story Of Wonder Dog

Dear Becky,

Dare to dream!

Richard R Stack

JOSH
The Story Of Wonder Dog

With A Little Help
From His Best Friend

Richard Lynn Stack

JOSH
The Story of Wonder Dog
Richard Lynn Stack

Also by Richard Lynn Stack:

The Doggonest Christmas
Illustrations by Charles W. Stack

The Doggonest Vacation
Illustrations by Sheri Lynn Mowrer

The Doggonest Puppy Love
Illustrations by Chet Phillips

Photography contributed by Debra Franson and many other friends and admirers of Josh.

Printed in U.S.A. by Taylor Publishing Company, Dallas, Texas.
Book produced by Neal Kimmel & Associates

Published and distributed by Windmill Press
7609 Beaver Road, Glen Burnie, Maryland 21060

ISBN 0-9628262-5-1

Dedicated to
Thomas Sooy, D.V.M.
Robert Etter, D.V.M.
and
Bob Carr & Nancy Cooper
without whom this book
would not be possible.

In 1983, a lawyer named Richard Stack was watching a Christmas movie at his home in Maryland. Richard felt that the story was teaching all the wrong things. He decided to write a book for children — one that would teach the right things, but also be fun to read.

So Richard wrote a story about a dog named Josh, a little mutt who dreamed of being important. Richard named his story *The Doggonest Christmas*.

Then Richard telephoned his uncle, Charles Stack, who is a gifted commercial artist. Richard asked his uncle if he would be willing to illustrate the book. Uncle Charles agreed to draw the pictures and asked Richard how he imagined his main character. Richard told him that *his* Josh would have long, red ears, a white face and lots of freckles.

But Uncle Charles drew Josh differently, and hoped that Richard would like his idea. When Richard was presented with the endearing picture, he thought that it was perfect.

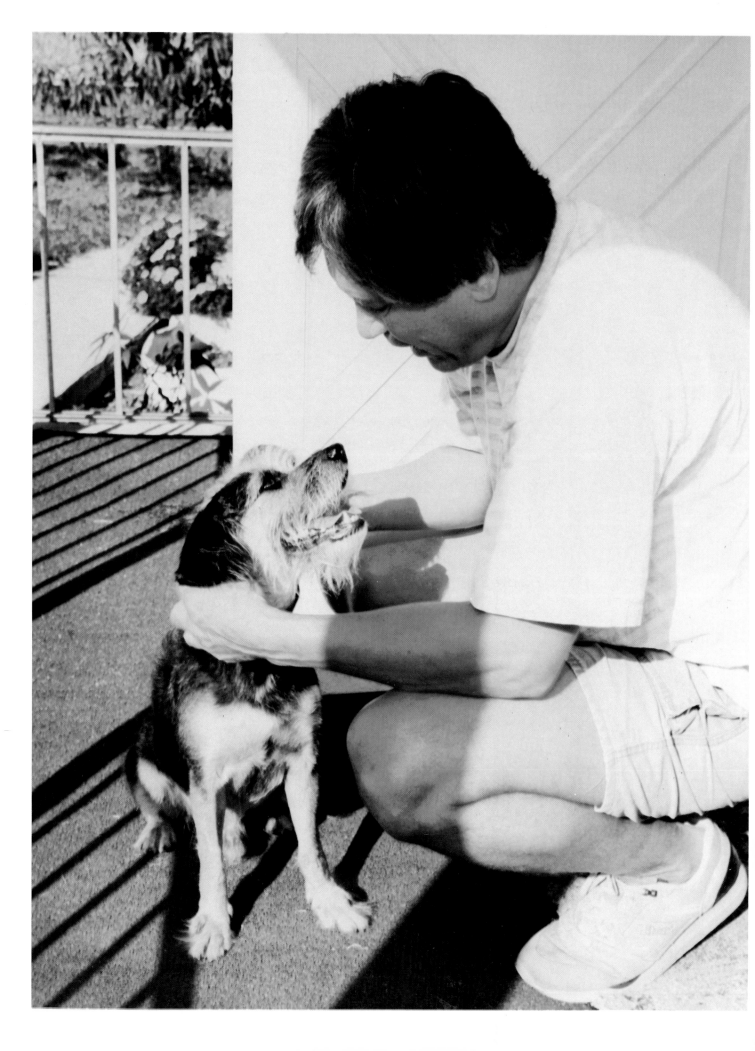

Then, something mysterious happened. A stray dog wearing an old brown collar wandered onto Richard's lawn. He  didn't belong to Richard's neighbors, and none of them knew where he had come from. He was not wearing a name tag or license, so the neighbors had nicknamed him "Butch." The dog looked just like the picture Uncle Charles had drawn! When he refused to go away, Richard adopted him, and named him "Josh."

Allow me to introduce myself. My name is Josh, and I'm the dog who wandered onto Richard's lawn. Actually, I adopted Richard — I just let him think that it was his idea. For a while, Richard wouldn't believe that I was meant to be his dog. I kept hanging around, but he still didn't catch on.

In Richard's office is an antique bank which belonged to his great-grandmother, Marie Brighoff. It is one of Richard's most-prized possessions. And it looks just like me! Uncle Charles' drawing and Grandma Brighoff's bank should have been enough to convince Richard. But sometimes he can be really dense. I realized that I would have to do something drastic to get through to him.

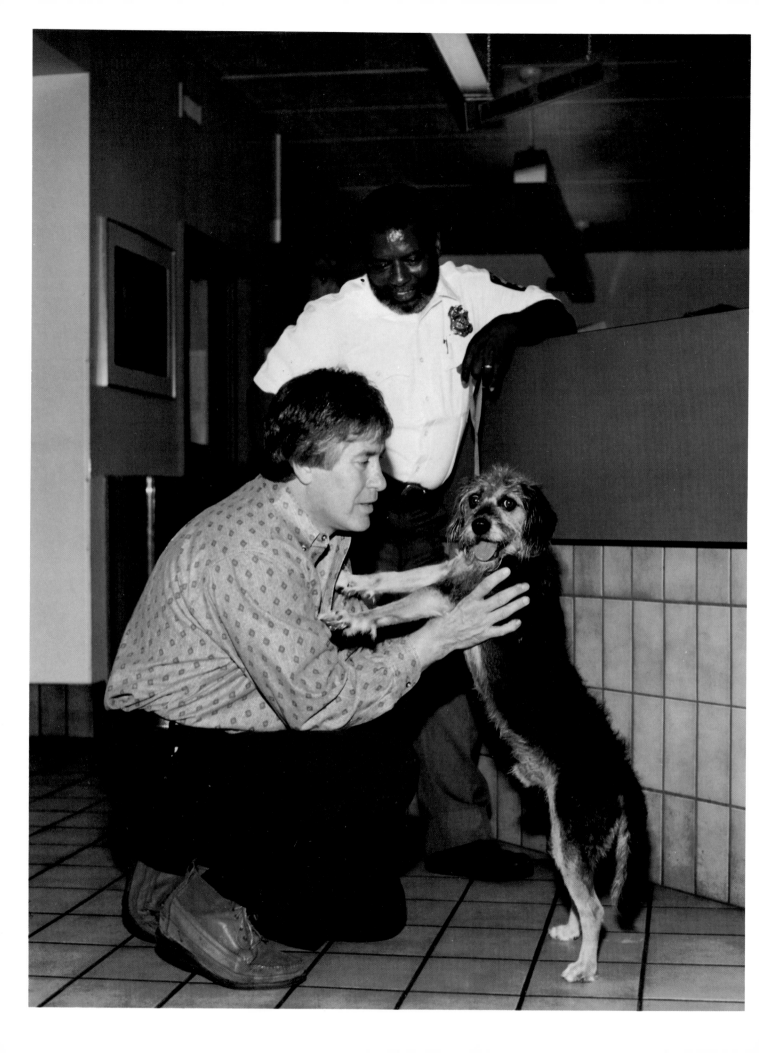

So I decided to get myself arrested. Well, not exactly *arrested*. But the animal control officer who locked me up sure did look like a sheriff. Then I sat waiting for Richard, and hoped that I hadn't made a big mistake. I was about three years old, and most people adopt dogs younger than  that. If Richard hadn't come after me, I could have been in serious trouble.

Well, I shouldn't have worried. Richard showed up, just the way I figured he would. I let out with some barking and howling that I'll bet is still echoing around that place. One of the "guards" took me to the front desk, where Richard was already bailing me out.

And that's how I adopted Richard.

Richard's mother, Anne Stack, still lives in the house where Richard grew up in Linthicum Heights, Maryland. She thinks of me as her grandson, and even calls herself my "Geemaw."

When Richard's father, Leon Stack, died in 1986, Geemaw was lonely and stayed at our home. I could tell that she needed extra loving, so at night, I'd sleep with Geemaw. I usually sleep on Richard's bed, but I knew that he would understand.

Geemaw has never forgotten the tenderness I showed her during that time. She loves me more than I can put into words. And she never gets tired of my company.

When Richard and I are traveling, Geemaw misses me immensely. When Richard telephones her, she always asks how I'm feeling. When we come back to Maryland, she hugs and kisses me even before she greets Richard. She always makes a big joke out of it. Grandmothers can be so much fun!

We live on Stoney Creek, in the community of Lombardee Beach. When I adopted Richard, I knew how lucky I was to have found him. Of all our neighbors, I probably have known Willie and Phylis Chambers the longest. They both have snow white hair, but I didn't give it to them.

A lot of my friends in the community are children. Richard thought it would be fun to have my picture taken with some of them. I thought it was more fun watching Richard trying to get everyone to hold still. I don't think he will ever be a child photographer.

When I came to live with Richard, I would run with my buddies, and visit the neighbors whenever I felt like it.

People always kept treats on hand, knowing that sooner or later I'd be dropping by. Now I can't go out by myself. One day, someone shot me with a gun.

I don't remember much about how I was shot. Perhaps it is too distressful for me to think about. But I have heard Richard talk about it many times. He says that in 1987, he went to Florida for the Christmas holidays. While he was away, Richard's secretaries and his good friend, Charlie Tufts, were baby-sitting for me.

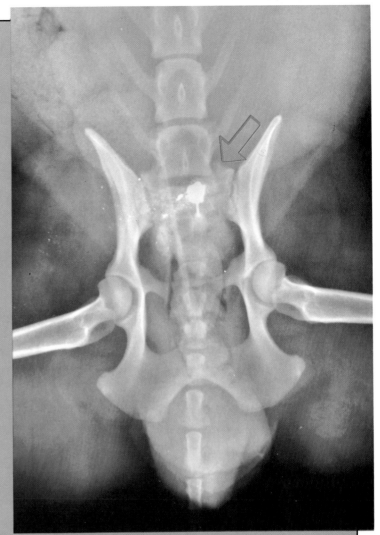

One morning, I began making my rounds of the community. When I didn't come home by that evening, Charlie and the secretaries became worried. They looked everywhere, but couldn't find me.

We have some neighbors named Bob Carr and Nancy Cooper. On Christmas Day, they went down to the water to check on their boats. Lying near their pier was a dog, and he seemed to be injured. Being tenderhearted people, Bob and Nancy took him to a veterinarian. X-rays revealed that the dog had been shot in the back.

Two days later, Bob and Nancy telephoned Richard's office. Someone had told them that the dog might belong to Richard. Charlie hurried over to see if I was the victim. There I was, feeling miserable, but very glad to see Charlie.

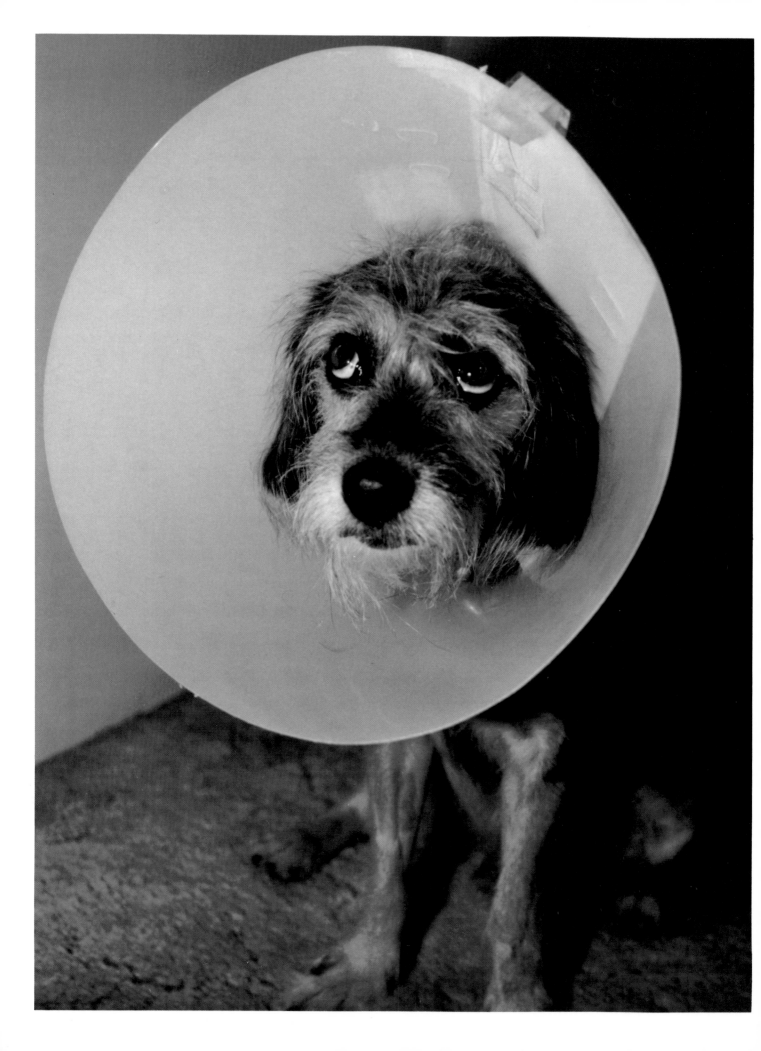

When Richard heard what had happened, he flew home from Florida. The bullet was still inside me, and I was in agony. So Richard had me examined by Dr. Tom Sooy, a highly-regarded neurosurgeon.

Dr. Sooy told Richard that I needed an operation to remove the bullet. He cautioned that even if I had the operation, I might never be able to walk again. He could only guess at what other problems I might be left with.

Richard says that he wanted to give me every chance to live. So with his permission, Dr. Sooy performed a delicate operation on me. Next to a ruler or pencil, the .22 caliber bullet he removed looks small. But when it was inside me, it felt like a cannonball.

After my operation, I had to wear a contraption that looks like a lamp shade. I felt ridiculous, but that was the least of my worries. The bullet had struck my spinal cord, where many nerves are located, and the pain was excruciating. Dr. Sooy said that everything humanly possible had been done for me.

While Richard had hoped to save my life, he could not bear to watch my suffering. After a lot of anguish and prayers, Richard arranged for Dr. Sooy to put me to sleep.

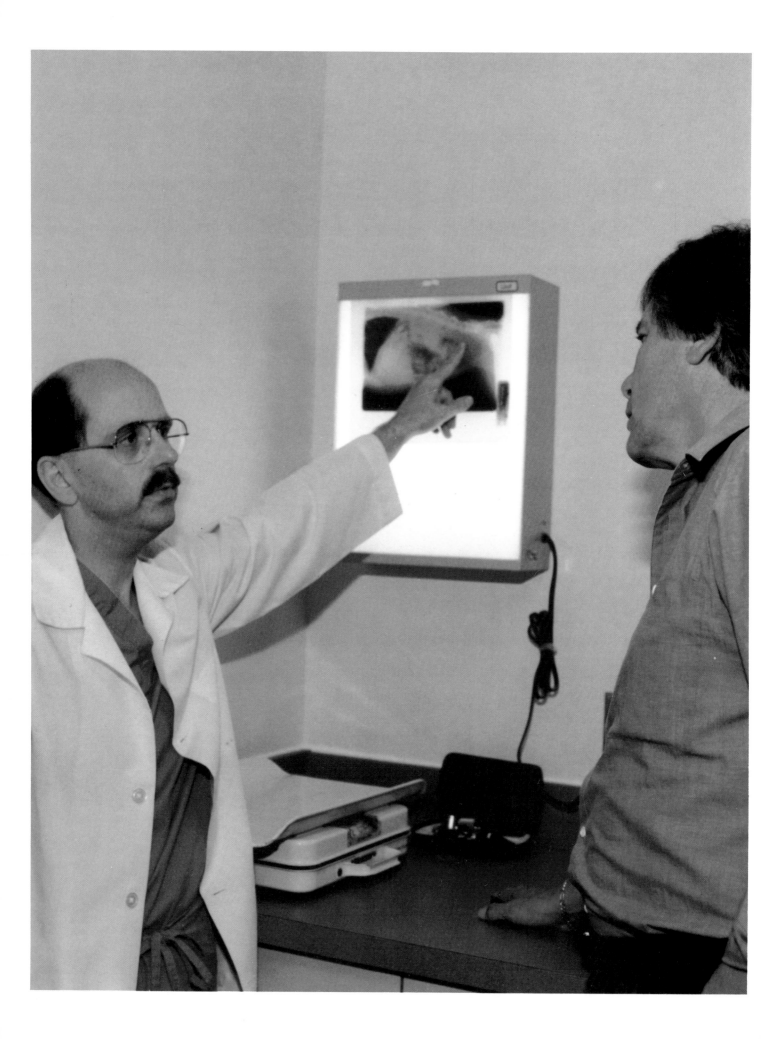

On the day my life was to end, Richard took me for one last walk in the community. He wanted me to have a chance to say good-bye to my other friends. People were hugging me. Some of them were crying.

As we were walking, something extraordinary happened — I began to feel better. Richard was dumbfounded by the sudden turnabout. Dr. Sooy was just as astonished, and could offer no explanation. Well, I kept getting better and better, and there was no more talk about ending my life.

The gunshot damaged some of my nerves, leaving me with problems that will never go away. I have difficulty going to the bathroom, so Richard helps me. He calls it "expressing my bladder." *I* call it squeezing my stomach! Also, my insides don't work the way they did before, so I have to eat a special diet.

Of all my problems, there is one that makes me saddest. I can't wag my tail anymore. But I consider how things might have turned out. And although Dr. Sooy was confounded by my dramatic recovery, there is an explanation which goes beyond medicine. Richard and I believe that our prayers were answered.

Now I only can dream of eating at McDonald's. I know that people food isn't good for dogs, but it would be especially harmful to me. Because of the gunshot, I now eat Hill's Prescription Diet — Canine c/d. I'm glad that I like it so well. But I must admit that I still like to pretend I'm "McDog" wolfing down a cheeseburger.

Since the bullet didn't paralyze me, I still can run and jump, and play games with Richard. Sometimes, he holds one end of an old sock in his teeth. I grab the other end with mine. Then we growl at each other and have a tug-of-war. Actually, I don't pull as hard as I could. My teeth are bigger and stronger than Richard's, and I don't want him to give up too easily. So I let him win once in a while.

When Richard has to leave me at home, I make up games that I can play by myself. I've found that even an empty box can be entertaining.

After *The Dog-gonest Christmas* was published in 1988, Richard worked hard to make it a success. I could see how important his book was to him.

Josh

And since he had done so much for me, I decided to show my gratitude. So when Richard was invited to autograph at book-stores, I went along to help him.

Right away, Richard could see that I was getting more attention than he was.

I hoped that he wouldn't be jealous. He wasn't, of course, and even let me autograph his books with my paw!

It came as a complete surprise to Richard the first time he was invited to speak at a school. Richard was *not* surprised, however, when he was asked to bring me with him.

I can still remember our first school visit. I was feeling laid-back, but Richard seemed a little nervous. He had experience speaking in courtrooms, but wasn't used to talking to children. So I made it easy for him — I let him talk about me. It must have worked, because we began to receive more and more requests for school visits.

HIGHLAND ELEMENTARY
THE DOGGONEST WELCOME TO AUTHOR RICHARD STACK & JOSH

It was becoming clear to me that Richard had an important message for children. I suggested that he devote himself to writing books and making school and library appearances. Richard had been practicing law for almost twenty years. In September 1989, he took my advice and closed his law practice. Then we headed out across the country, appearing together at schools and libraries in other states.

HILL VIEW ELEMENTARY
A BIG WELCOME TO RICHARD AND JOSH WE LOVE YOUR BOOKS!

Since 1989, Richard and I have been on the road thirty-five weeks a year. We travel in a big motorhome; Richard calls it the "world's biggest doghouse." So far, we have been to thirty-nine states, and have appeared at more than a thousand schools and libraries.

At each school or library, everyone is given the opportunity to pet me. Richard believes that I have been petted more than any dog in history. He hopes that *The Guinness Book of World Records* will recognize me as the most-petted dog in the world. I am, even if Mr. Guinness doesn't admit it.

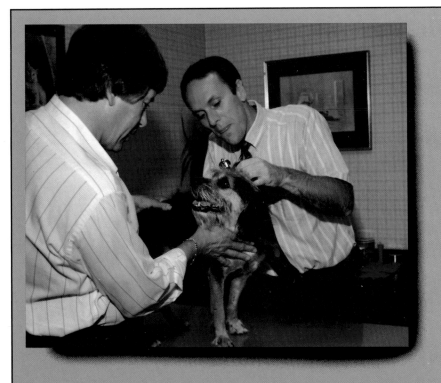

Richard makes sure that I always have the best medical care. My veterinarian is Dr. Robert Etter, a friend of Dr. Sooy. Dr. Etter and his staff at Pasadena Animal Hospital think that I am wonderful. I do have to admit that they think all their clients are wonderful.

Richard and I have confidence in Dr. Etter's ability. He has operated on me for bladder stones, removed lumps from my paw, ear and back, and neutered me. He has even cleaned my teeth!

Occasionally, I may need medical care while Richard and I are traveling. So Richard keeps copies of my medical and vaccination records on board the motorhome. He also brings the X-rays that were taken when I was shot. And if necessary, another veterinarian can confer with Dr. Etter by telephone.

I have a beautiful girlfriend named Sneakers. She is twice as big as I am, but that doesn't matter to me. She likes me, and not just because I'm a star. She doesn't even mind that I can't wag my tail.

Sneakers lives in Viewpoint Beach, not far from our house. I could walk to her house in no time at all, if Richard would still let me. Before I was shot, I would visit Sneakers whenever I wanted. Now I have to wait for Richard to take me for walks, and convince him to go by her house.

Sneakers is quite an athlete. Once Richard and I met her at the community playground. She showed us how to use the merry-go-round and sliding board. I had a great time riding the merry-go-round with Sneakers, but Richard wouldn't let me near the sliding board. I think he was afraid that I might break my leg or something. I know Richard was just looking out for me, but I wanted to show off a little bit for my girlfriend.

STATE OF MARYLAND

·PROCLAMATION·

From the Governor of Maryland, William Donald Schaefer

JOSH, THE WONDER DOG DAY
DECEMBER 24, 1992

WHEREAS, Throughout the annals of Maryland history, dogs have been cherished and respected as "man's best friend", providing love, protection and friendship for countless families and individuals in our communities; and

WHEREAS, Anne Arundel County is home to a very special dog, celebrity and star of television, radio and books who has inspired his peers and human beings alike in unique and powerful ways, and his name is indeed most fitting and appropriate for a loyal canine that has had to endure and overcome a great deal in his short life - "Josh, The Wonder Dog"; and

WHEREAS, Shot by an unknown assailant six years ago to this very day, Josh survived such a brutal assault thanks to the devoted efforts of his highly skilled doctors, the prayers of his many friends, and by his own courage and determination; and

WHEREAS, Since that time, Josh has been dedicated to spreading the valuable message of self-belief by visiting hundreds of schools across the country - earning the tremendous respect of children, educators and our public at-large while gaining recognition and acclaim as the most petted dog in the world; and

WHEREAS, Maryland is pleased to join with his proud owner, author Richard L. Stack, in saluting Josh, The Wonder Dog... and in wishing Josh the best of good health and success in the years ahead as he continues to build upon his legacy of caring and outreach.

NOW, THEREFORE, I, WILLIAM DONALD SCHAEFER, GOVERNOR OF THE STATE OF MARYLAND, do hereby proclaim December 24, 1992 as JOSH, THE WONDER DOG DAY in Maryland, and do commend this observance to all of our citizens.

Given Under My Hand and the Great Seal of the State of Maryland,
this **24th** *day of* **December**
One Thousand Nine Hundred and **Ninety-two**

William Donald Schaefer
Governor

Secretary of State

The State of Maryland has bestowed upon me a very special honor. Governor William Donald Schaefer has proclaimed December 24th to be *Josh, The Wonder Dog Day*. In 1992, my proclamation was presented to me by State Senator Phil Jimeno and his family. It is Senator Jimeno who made my day possible. He and his family were genuinely happy for me, and made me feel important.

Richard believes that the attention I receive is meaningful for children. He says that children often give up easily, or don't try because they are afraid of failure. Richard says that if he can make me into a star, children may be inspired to do their best. After all, I was an unwanted stray with no pedigree, was shot and now have serious health problems.

So Richard finds ways to make me famous. It takes hard work to make dreams come true.

Because of Richard's efforts, I have become a 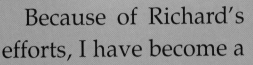 celebrity. I have appeared on television more than eighty times, been featured in hundreds of newspapers stories, and even talked on the radio. In Baltimore, WBAL talk show host Alan Prell called me a "publicity hound!"

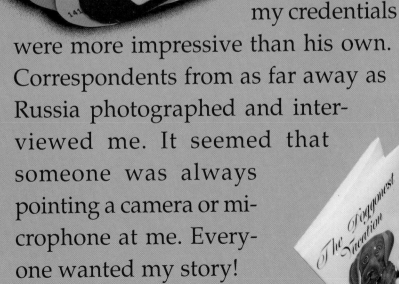

In 1992, I was invited to the Republican National Convention in Houston. I was given special tags to wear so President Bush would know I didn't sneak in. One reporter remarked that my credentials were more impressive than his own. Correspondents from as far away as Russia photographed and interviewed me. It seemed that someone was always pointing a camera or microphone at me. Everyone wanted my story!

Being in the public eye means I have to take a lot of baths. It should be understood that I *detest* baths. I've been known to go through a screen door when I hear water running. Richard calls a bath "the B word," as if I won't catch on!

At home, Richard had a special shower built in the master bathroom. I knew I was in trouble when I saw the plumber installing some shower heads down low where I am. Richard wasn't fooling me one bit!

Well, I decided that when I have to take a bath, Richard should also. I hear people say that we should not waste water. So I figure if we both get wet, we'll be getting more from the water we are using. I don't think that Richard agrees with my way of thinking.

Miss Noller's class enjoyed...

THE DOGGONEST CHRISTMAS

In 1991, while visiting schools near Atlanta, Georgia, I decided to make another change in Richard's life. He was forty-eight years old, but had never been married. Since my heart belonged to Sneakers, I felt that Richard should have a true love of his own.

One rainy January day, we visited McKendree Elementary School, in the little town of Lawrenceville. While we were at the school, Richard was captivated by a very pretty teacher named Marla Noller. Richard still thinks that he noticed her without my help. But it was I who made her turn around for a moment, so that he could catch a glimpse of her long, beautiful hair. It's my secret how I did it.

That afternoon, Richard asked Marla if she would go out to dinner with him. I was excited when she accepted his invitation, but jealous when they didn't take me with them. Even without my company, they must have enjoyed themselves. They went out three more times before Richard and I left town.

Eight weeks later, Richard flew to Georgia to spend Easter weekend with Marla and her family. When he returned from his visit, I learned that Richard and Marla were going to be married. On Easter morning, Richard had proposed to Marla atop Stone Mountain. I wasn't at all surprised. It happened just the way I planned it.

On August 10, 1991, Marla and Richard were married at St. John Lutheran Church in Linthicum Heights. Since their marriage was my idea, they decided that I should participate in the wedding. I was listed in the program as "Best Friend." Eddie Rossiter, the handsome Ring Bearer, escorted me to my seat in the second row, right behind Geemaw. I'm glad that she is short. Otherwise, I wouldn't have been able to see what was happening.

The wedding ceremony was performed by Pastor William Gilroy and Pastor Carl Folkemer. I was flabbergasted when I heard Pastor Gilroy's sermon. He called me a "special guest" and recounted how

I had brought Richard and Marla together. I was so very proud!

After the wedding, Richard and Marla spent their honeymoon traveling in Egypt, Greece and Turkey. I know they

were disappointed when I decided not to go with them. But the temperature over there in August is sweltering, and I would have found it unbearable. Anyway, the newlyweds needed some time alone to get to know each other better.

So now I have two people to take care of, but I don't mind one bit. It's a lot of work, but I get twice as much loving. The dedication of *The Doggonest Puppy Love* says it best:

"Dedicated to Marla June Stack,
who loves Josh, The Wonder Dog,
almost as much as the author."

And I'll bet my last dog biscuit that Marla and Richard will live happily ever after — with my help, of course. Wow, Oh Bow Wow!

The
ABSOLUTE BEGINNER'S GUIDE TO
PATCHWORK
QUILTING
&
APPLIQUÉ

Elaine Hammond

David & Charles

To Robbit, my husband and best friend, with thanks for his love and pride – it is life blood to me.
To Laura and Briony, my lovely girls, my fiercest critics and staunchest supporters.
To my parents, Brian and Shirley Baty, who from my earliest days have been a solid and loving example and very dear friends. They are the best, and together with my sisters, Andy and Jill, have helped me make several dreams a reality.
Thank you for your belief in me even when I doubted myself.

Detail from under the Sea Cushion (page 76)

A DAVID & CHARLES BOOK

First published in the UK in 1997

Text and designs Copyright © Elaine Hammond 1997
Photography and layout Copyright © David & Charles 1997

A catalogue record for this book is available from the British Library.

ISBN 0 7153 0479 8

Photography by Paul Biddle
Book design by Roger Daniels
Illustrations by Terry Evans
Printed in Great Britain
by Butler & Tanner Ltd
for David & Charles
Brunel House   Newton Abbot   Devon

Contents

Introduction

I was lucky enough to discover patchwork and quilting twenty years ago. Then, however, there was little information available and what there was seemed so alien that I, in my wisdom, chose to ignore many instructions. My first attempt at piecing resulted in a fairly acceptable cushion for my mother's rocking chair, so, flushed with success, I made a tea-cosy. Now I considered myself to be quite an expert, so the next logical step would be to make a double bed-size quilt for my brother-in-law's wedding – wouldn't it?

That first quilt was a disaster, not least because I ignored the instructions. However my enthusiasm was undimmed, so I carried on with small pieces, attending workshops whenever and wherever I could, and absorbing information like a sponge. Desire to be involved makes learning easy and I found my knowledge increasing almost effortlessly. Through all this however, I found myself drawn to basic books of instruction, where clear diagrams and pictures enabled me to create without reading great screeds of text first. My quilting life would have had a much faster growth if I hadn't had to glean information here and there instead of having one book to help with the three related crafts of patchwork, quilting and appliqué. I have tried to make this book work in the same way. You will find the section on Materials and Equipment most useful, helping you to decide what equipment to get – though very little is really required. The text with the most information is collected in the Basic Techniques section and here you will find the techniques and stitches clearly laid out. This is followed by over twenty-five attractive projects.

Beautiful combinations of patchwork, quilting and appliqué in the Ring Cushion (page 104), the Cathedral Window Album Cover (page 108) and the Double Wedding Ring Wall Hanging (page 111)

Celtic tea-cosy and pot holder (page 72).

Patchwork is a fascinating and versatile craft. I am sure most quilters are asked why they feel the need to cut up pieces of fabric and stitch them together again. In truth, it is sometimes hard to explain. Some people are fascinated by the geometry and the satisfaction of creating an entirely new design where all the pieces actually fit together. Some find patchwork an ideal way to 'play' with colours, combining them to create further spectrum ranges and individual statements. In this book I introduce you to many patchwork techniques. The projects are straightforward and you will learn a lot from them, but you will also be left with a grounding in each technique. For example, instead of the Cathedral Window Album Cover, you could make a cushion or bag.

Quilting is a beautiful technique which, in the main, uses one simple stitch. Yet from this comes some of the most sublime needlework to be found anywhere. Originally employed as simply a means of holding three layers of material together for warmth, quilting has become a stunning art form in its own right. I have introduced quilting in various forms in this book: on its own as seen in the Devon Dumpling Cot Quilt; with appliqué, as in the Spring Basket Wall Hanging, and of course in conjunction with patchwork, shown in many of the projects such as the Scrumpy Quilt.

Appliqué is a decorative technique rather than a functional one. There are several methods for various uses, and again the results can be breathtaking. There are no limits to the images and designs you can create with this technique. It can be used for fun, such as in the Gingerbread Apron and Bag; as symbolism, as seen in the Ring Cushion or for a decorative function, as in the Country-Style Tree Skirt.

The projects have been chosen to be useful, appealing and instructive and you should have a good working knowledge of patchwork, quilting and appliqué by the end of the book. I am sure you will also be excited by the sheer versatility of these three techniques and be keen to move on to even more creative ideas. If this is so, I will have succeeded in my main aim – to introduce these fascinating crafts to beginners, in the hope that they will get as much enjoyment out of them as I have. The layout of the book has been designed for maximum ease of use. The projects are described in simple, easy-to-follow steps, accompanied by photographs and line drawings. Where a specific technique is involved, a page reference shows you where to go in the Basic Techniques section, where it is clearly described.

So here you have it, the book I would have liked twenty years ago. If you are a beginner quilter I hope you find it useful, but I would also encourage you to join a quilters' group and visit exhibitions. In many ways I envy you, you have a wonderful, rich voyage of discovery ahead. Enjoy it!

Materials and Equipment

Patchwork, quilting and appliqué are crafts which need very little equipment. The most important element is the fabric, followed by the threads. Of course there is a wealth of gadgetry available, but not all of it is necessary. It is much better to start with the basics and add more as you come across useful ideas. Descriptions of the basic equipment and how to use them follow in alphabetical order.

Awl or paper punch This is a very useful tool, ideal for punching neat holes where required, either on card or when small holes are needed within a particular project.

Basic sewing kit A small box or bag containing the items featured in the box, right and illustrated in the photograph below.

Beeswax This is used to wax and strengthen ordinary sewing thread for quilting when quilting thread of the desired colour is unavailable.

BASIC SEWING KIT

Needles – quilting and sharps for hand sewing.
Scissors – for paper and thread/fabric.
Threads – neutral for most sewing and coloured for current projects.
Thimble.
Tape measure.
Pins, safety pins and pincushion.
Ruler – 15cm (6in) and 30cm (12in).
Pencil and pen.

Bias bars These are metal or heat-resistant plastic bars available in a range of sizes. The bars are used to hold tape straight when pressing bias strips for appliqué.

Bias binding This is binding cut on the diagonal or cross of the fabric grain. It gives the strip elasticity and so is particularly useful for binding curves.

Bondaweb (see Fusible web)

Cardboard Never throw cereal boxes away! Keep the front and back pieces as they are very useful for making templates for patchwork, quilting and appliqué. Birthday cards and card pieces from tights packets are also useful.

Compasses Relics from the school geometry set, compasses are used for creating circular designs for patchwork, quilting and appliqué.

Cutting mat These mats are made of a special material which has 'self-healing' properties. They are available in various sizes and are well worth the investment as they will prolong the life of rotary cutter blades and will help protect your work surfaces.

Edging band This is useful for extending the edges of a piece of work to enable you to work right to the edge when using a hoop or frame. Use old sheeting or spare fabric. You need three or four pieces approximately 31cm (12in) wide and 1–1.5m (1–1½yd) long. Neaten the raw edges by hemming or zigzag stitching. Used double, they can be pinned to the edge of the quilt to extend it.

Fabrics Patchwork, quilting and appliqué can be made from most fabrics though some are easier to handle than others. Generally, 100% cotton fabrics are the easiest and most satisfying, holding a crease well. It is best to wash your fabrics as soon as you buy them, individually in mild soap, then rinsing

---

ESSENTIAL EQUIPMENT

basic sewing kit
paper – plain, graph and isometric
15cm (6in) and 30cm (12in) rulers
colouring pencils and marking pencils
felt-tip pens
glue stick
hoop or frame
templates
card – medium-thickness

well. Note how colourfast a fabric is at the same time. If it persistently 'bleeds' you should discard it, because it will probably ruin a project. Dry fabrics naturally or gently in a dryer, press them and store in a clean box.

Fusible web This is basically a fine web of glue on a paper backing. Apart from strengthening fabrics it is used mostly for appliqué (see full instructions for use on page 25). Bondaweb is a brand name for fusible webbing produced by Vilene.

Glue Thick, multi-purpose glue such as Copydex is useful for gluing card, paper and fabric and is particularly useful for projects such as fabric-covered boxes.

Glue sticks are useful for making templates and for gluing paper sheets together to make larger areas. They can also be used to temporarily hold fabric pieces in place.

Graph paper This is used for drafting designs. Templates can be drafted on to graph paper, then cut out and stuck to medium-weight card. Isometric graph paper is excellent for drafting hexagonal designs.

Knitting needle or plastic swizzle stick These are useful implements for ensuring that the seams, corners and points are smooth and well-defined when you turn fabric through to the right side. They also help to stuff wadding into small spaces as in trapunto and corded quilting (where you insert stuffing or cord into

pre-sewn shapes and channels). A large cable needle is also useful.

Light box A light box is a purpose-built box with a transparent sheet of perspex or glass over a light source, to which the quilting or appliqué design is taped. The integral light illuminates the design from below, making it easier to see and trace. You can, however, create a simple light box by taping your design to a well-lit window or by using a glass-topped table with a lamp below it, or even a tea chest with a light inside and a glass or clear plastic top.

Masking tape Available in various widths, the most useful being 0.5cm (¼in) and 2.5cm (1in), masking tape is excellent for marking quilting lines.

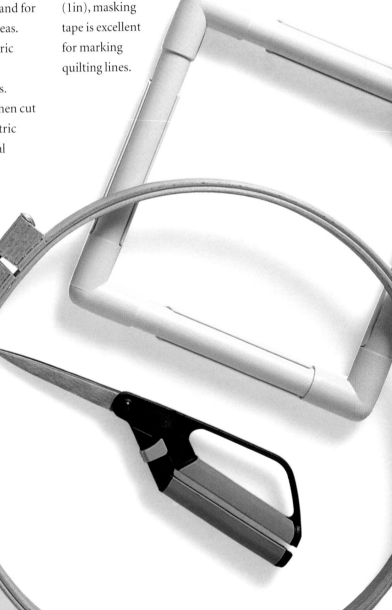

Simply stick the masking tape to the quilt top, mark along its edge, then peel it off. It is also useful when quilting long straight lines such as grids. Stick it along your quilt top when it is in the hoop or frame to mark your quilting line. Quilt alongside it, then remove the tape. Each piece of tape can be used two or three times. Use masking tape to hold fabrics and paper temporarily in place, especially to a window to trace designs.

Needles You will need a variety of needles. For piecing try 'sharps'; for quilting use 'betweens'. These are short and fine and may seem impossibly small to start with. Start with a size 8 or 9 and progress to a 10 or even 12 (the smaller the needle, the higher the number). Blunt tapestry needles are useful for marking quilting designs by piercing and for corded and trapunto quilting (where stuffing or cord is inserted into pre-sewn shapes and channels). Large doll-making needles help to make tacking up a quilt much easier.

Ornamentation Feel free to use all sorts of embellishments – buttons, beads, charms and so on – on your projects, particularly on wall hangings or clothing (though for safety reasons **not** on quilts to be used by small children or babies). The addition of gold beads for example will add a glow to your work. Buttons are useful for tying quilts and also for adding a touch of whimsy, while charms, beads and sequins will add visual appeal.

Pencils and pens *Pencils* are needed for design work and marking out. Hard graphite pencils and silver and gold colouring pencils are used to mark quilt tops; softer graphite pencils are best for drawing around templates.

Coloured pencils are ideal for deciding colour choices. Use them to colour in your drawn patchwork designs to experiment. Remember that dark colours tend to recede, while light colours are thrown forward. Coloured pencils are also useful for marking quilting designs on fabric. Choose a colour slightly darker than the fabric and mark lightly. The stitches will cover the marks.

Felt-tip pens can also colour your design ideas, bringing them to life.

Marking pens are available in many types, so experiment to find which suit you best. For some projects, particularly those that will be washed, water-erasable marking pens are ideal. Graphite and coloured pencils also make excellent markers.

Pins and pincushion *Dressmaking pins* will be needed for holding fabric together when piecing or doing appliqué work. Invest in some good, fine ones. Those with glass heads are easier to find in folds of fabric. Choose your pins according to what fabric you are using.

Safety pins can be used to hold your quilt sandwich together. When machine quilting this means you can remove each pin as you get to it, and there are no threads

USEFUL EQUIPMENT

0.5cm (¼in) wide masking tape
beeswax
bias bars
compasses
safety pins
sewing machine
template plastic

ADDITIONAL EQUIPMENT

large rotary cutter
rotary ruler
self-healing cutting mat
special sewing machine feet
stencils – painting and quilting

Hand-held frames are available in wood or plastic. The wooden ones are suitable for projects such as cushion tops, the piece being stitched onto canvas strips on all four inner edges.

Plastic clip frames are the best frames by far and are available in several sizes. A plastic clip frame consists of a square of plastic tubing and four plastic clips. The wadded quilting is put over the square and clipped into place. You can increase the tension by gripping the clips on two sides and turning outwards, or relieve the tension by turning inwards. Light and comfortable to hold, these frames can be dismantled for storage and removed at night to allow the fabric to rest.

Quilting hoops These are available in various sizes and consist of two rings of wood, rather like embroidery hoops but with deeper sides. The best size for most

for your machine foot to catch. Safety pins can also be used in place of ordinary pins when you want your work to be held quite firmly.

Pincushions help to keep pins sharp and you are less likely to stab yourself if you don't have to dip into a box of pins.

Quilting frames Quilting frames are very helpful in making sure you achieve an even quilting tension, and that the stitches are the same size front and back. There are several sorts of quilting frame.

Floor frames are usually large with rollers at each side. The quilt is stitched onto canvas attached to the roller and then the rollers are evenly turned until the quilt is taut enough for stitching. The rollers are turned to move on to the next area to be stitched.

people is 36cm (14in) diameter. This enables you to quilt a fairly large area easily without straining your shoulders. The quilt is placed over the smaller hoop, then the larger hoop is placed over the quilt. Tightening the screw holds the three layers securely in place and provides tension on the quilt surface, making it easier to quilt. The disadvantage of a quilting hoop is the fact that it is round, which means you will get some stretch on the bias where the hoop is tight on the quilt. However, providing you take the hoop off the quilt overnight (or if you are not quilting for some time) this should not be too much of a problem.

Rotary cutter A rotary cutter saves hours of laborious cutting with scissors and is especially useful if you have dozens of fabric pieces to cut. It is a tool rather like a pizza cutter, with a very sharp, round blade and a built-in blade guard. Because the blade rolls along the fabric, the line cut is continuous, clear and straight. A quilt top can be cut out in hours rather than days and this time-saving alone makes it well worth investigating. For efficient use, the rotary cutter should be used with a self-healing cutting mat and a rotary ruler, and the combined expense can be quite considerable, so it is worth requesting a demonstration at a quilt shop. After the initial cost, you will only need to buy replacement blades when necessary.

Rulers Keep standard 15cm (6in) and 30cm (12in) rulers in your basic sewing kit. They will be useful for both drafting designs and marking quilts.

Rotary rulers are made of thick transparent acrylic material and are designed to be used with a rotary cutter. There are several makes available and all are clearly marked with inches, with some now available in centimetres. They are also available in different sizes. The best size to start with is 24×6in, which have ¼in and ⅛in divisions clearly marked. This enables you to spread your hand safely on top of the ruler. You then press down on the ruler while the rotary cutter blade glides along the thick edge of it, enabling you to cut safely and accurately.

Scissors You should have three pairs of scissors – one solely for paper, one for fabric and small ones for threads. Choose comfortable, sharp scissors and keep them exclusively for your patchwork, quilting and appliqué.

Seam unpicker This tool is not the pessimistic item it may seem. Of course there will be times when you need to unpick stitches, but this tool is also useful for stuffing small areas, in trapunto quilting for example. It also acts as a useful guide when machine piecing as the unpicker can be used sideways to guide the fabrics under the foot of the sewing machine.

Sewing machine Although many patchwork projects have to be made by hand, it is well worth investing in a sewing machine to free you from some of the drudgery of sewing. It does not have to be anything fancy or brand-new – zigzag stitches are about the most refined you will need for patchwork.

Special sewing machine feet are well worth the investment if you intend to use your machine regularly for patchwork, quilting and appliqué. There are two very useful ones. The first is a foot with an accurate ¼in side. For example, Bernina make a patchwork foot No. 37, designed for machine piecing. Other manufacturers have similar products available, making it much easier to machine piece accurately. For machine quilters, the walking foot is a worthwhile investment. This tool helps to feed two or more layers of fabric under the needle together at the same time. This helps to prevent the puckering of the bottom layer which can plague the machine quilter.

Stencils These are available for quilting and painting. You can stencil a design onto plain fabric and quilt around the motif, or choose a suitable quilting stencil to mark your quilt top. If there is a small, regular repeating pattern, in a square in the middle of a patchwork block for example, you can mark the design on your work just before you quilt it, when it is already in the frame.

Templates *Commercial templates* are available for

quilting and appliqué and are a good choice in many cases, since the precision laser-cut kind are very accurate. They are quite expensive however, and will probably only be worthwhile if you plan to get a lot of use out of them.

Home-made templates are easily constructed in cardboard or plastic. The choice of material used can depend on the intended project. Template plastic (available from patchwork materials suppliers) is a good choice for a big project where many pieces are needed. Card will wear down with repeated use, whereas plastic will not. But if you are only going to use a template a few times, medium-weight card will be fine.

Thimble Although when you first wear one, a thimble can seem really unwieldy, prolonged sewing without one will soon convince you of its usefulness. Make sure it fits – you should not be able to feel it when you are wearing it. There are many designs available in leather, plastic, metal and china. Just experiment until you find what is best for you.

Threads For most patchwork projects, cotton thread is most appropriate since cotton fabric is generally used. For patchwork, try to use a neutral-coloured thread especially when sewing scrap quilts where lots of different coloured fabrics are being used. It is much easier to use a mid-grey which will tone with most fabrics. For tacking, keep a lightweight light-coloured thread in your workbox for both quilt 'sandwiches' and smaller projects. Again, 100% cotton thread is best. For quilting, there are specialist quilting threads available in a range of colours. These are thicker than average thread with a finish that is less likely to tangle. For quilting it is more important that the threads be the right colour. If you can't find the right colour, ordinary cotton thread pulled through beeswax to add strength and smoothness is a suitable substitute – indeed many quilters prefer it anyway.

Wadding There are several types and weights of wadding. It is available in polyester, polyester/cotton, cotton and wool, and in weights from 2–6oz, though there are 'low loft' fleeces available which are less than 2oz and useful for clothes or small quilts. There are also really thick waddings used for duvets and sleeping bags, but they are not usually used for quiltmaking. In general the 2oz weight is the popular choice. It is often most cost effective to buy bed-size pieces of wadding. You can then cut pieces from it and it will also save time since you won't have to piece together lengths for a bed quilt.

Polyester is the cheapest and most versatile choice for wadding, and is used for quilts and clothing. It is easily worked, does not need to be too closely quilted and will wash well, a bonus particularly for projects such as cot quilts. There are two major disadvantages with polyester wadding. It has the annoying habit of 'bearding' – this is where small fibres work their way through the top layer of the quilt and give it a furry appearance. There is nothing you can do about this after it happens, though you can try to minimise it by buying a bonded wadding, which has a surface designed to contain the fibres. You can also buy dark wadding as well as white, and the darker one should be chosen for darker fabrics. The other disadvantage is that the wadding flattens with use, and once lost, it will never regain the 'spring' of a new piece of work.

Polyester/cotton is a useful wadding, particularly for machine quilting and work requiring a flatter, more old-fashioned look and feel. It can be machine washed, often resulting in shrinkage which adds to the antique look.

Cotton is quite heavy and needs to be quilted thoroughly in order to hold the fibres together, and the finished quilt will be heavy and difficult to wash. However cotton wadding is a popular choice for machine quilters since the resulting quilt will be flat and firm.

Wool is the perfect choice for making an heirloom quilt. It is light, springy and soft, and will retain these properties through a long life. The main drawback with wool wadding is the cost as it is generally more expensive than the alternatives.

Basic Techniques

The projects in this book have some general techniques in common, covering the basic aspects of patchwork, quilting and appliqué. These are described in full here and referenced in each of the projects as necessary.

ENLARGING PATTERNS

Enlarging patterns is often necessary and can be done using a photocopier, most of which have percentage facilities. If the enlargement required is greater than the maximum percentage the photocopier allows, you will need to copy the design once, selecting the greatest available enlargement, and then copy your copy again, enlarging it to the correct size. Copying templates in this way can cause subtle distortions, so it is worth checking that the copied paper templates fit together correctly before cutting any fabric.

Sometimes it is only possible to show a half or quarter of a symmetrical quilting pattern. In this case you will need to enlarge the pattern as instructed and then trace it off once (for a half pattern) or three times (for a quarter pattern) before assembling the pieces to make a pattern for the whole design.

USING A LIGHT BOX

The integral light source in a light box (see equipment, page 11) illuminates a design, making it easier to see and trace. You can mimic a commercial light box by taping your design to a well-lit window (or by using a glass-topped table or tea-chest with a lamp below) and then carefully copying the design. (See also, marking out a design, page 21.)

ROTARY CUTTING

To use a rotary cutter, first press your fabrics and layer them, either several pieces together or one piece folded so there are four to six layers. Place your ruler on top and, pressing firmly on your ruler with one hand to keep it stable, cut along the ruler edge with the cutter, pressing fairly hard and pushing the blade away from you. Because a rotary cutter blade is so sharp you *must* get used to replacing the guard each time you use it. There are lots of ready-made acrylic templates available for rotary cutting and many books which show speed piecing quilt blocks taking full advantage of the rotary cutter.

ENGLISH PAPER PIECING

This is a patchwork technique using papers cut to the exact size of the patchwork pieces required. It is useful for shapes such as small hexagons or diamonds.

1 First, make a template of medium-thickness card the exact size you wish your shape to be – this will be for the papers. Now make another the same shape but 0.5cm (¼in) bigger all round – this will be for the fabric pieces and allows for seams.

2 Using the smaller template cut several 'papers' from fairly stiff paper – old photocopies are fine, tissue paper is not. Then cut your fabrics using the larger template.

3 Pin a paper shape to the middle of a fabric shape, then fold the fabric around the paper and tack into place, as shown in Fig.1. Repeat with all the fabric shapes.

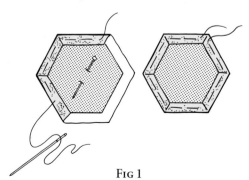

FIG 1

4 Place two shapes right sides together, oversew along the seam, then add the next shape and oversew and so on (see Fig.2).

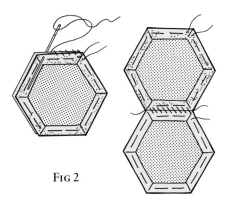

FIG 2

5 When the design is completed, remove the tacking and papers.

HAND PIECING

This way of patchworking usually begins with the making of a template. This is then followed by the process of marking and cutting the fabric, pinning pieces together, assembling blocks, then hand stitching, pressing and finally joining rows.

Making and Using Templates

Templates for patchwork, particularly hand-pieced work, should be made of durable material since you will re-use each template many times for one quilt. The usual materials for making templates are plastic or medium-weight card. Once made, templates are best stored in a clear plastic grip-seal bag, with the name and size of the block clearly marked.

To make a template in plastic Place the plastic over the template shape and, using a ruler and fine marker pen, trace off the relevant line (see Seam Allowance Rule opposite), making sure the corners are clearly marked. Mark the straight grain, number or letter, the name of the block, where possible, and 1 of 5, 2 of 5 and so on, where relevant. Then cut out the shape using sharp scissors, craft knife or a rotary cutter. If you have a cutter with a blade that is getting too blunt for fabric, keep it for cardboard and plastic.

To make a template in card Trace your design onto paper. Glue it with Copydex or a glue stick to medium-weight card (cereal packet card is excellent for this). Then using sharp scissors or a rotary cutter, cut out the shape.

Marking and Cutting Fabric

Marking and cutting fabric are important steps in patchwork, quilting and appliqué. First decide the straight grain of your fabric and make sure that you place your template on it. The straight grain runs parallel to the selvedge (the edge of the fabric). If you don't follow the straight grain as directed, the patchwork pieces may distort as you sew them. Sometimes the marked straight grain will mean your template seems crooked on the fabric, but there is a reason for this – trust the designer of the block!

Using a sharp pencil, draw a line around your template, taking extra care to make sure the corners

SEAM ALLOWANCE RULE

Most of the templates in this book have marked on them an inner (sewing) line and outer (cutting) line which includes a seam allowance.

When you cut the templates for machine piecing you should include the seam allowances, cutting out the templates to the outer (dotted) line. The width of the sewing machine foot will automatically allow 0.5cm (¼in) between the cut edge and the sewing line. Check the width of your presser foot to make sure of this.

For hand piecing, the seam allowances should *not* be included. Cut out the template to the inner (solid) line. Place the template on the fabric and draw around it. This drawn line becomes the sewing line. Cut out the fabric piece allowing a 0.5cm (¼in) seam allowance from the drawn line. You will be surprised by how quickly you can learn to do this by eye.

are clear – this will help when you are piecing. Allow approximately 1.25cm (½in) between the pieces so you can easily cut them out. If in doubt, leave more – you can always trim it later, but you can't add it on. Mark all the pieces on one fabric before cutting to be sure you have enough fabric. Cut out approximately halfway between pieces, trimming the excess later.

Pinning

You can pin your pieces together in two ways. Try both, then stick with the one you prefer.

❖ Hold the pieces right sides together, place a pin through the corner points, flipping the pieces over as you go to check they match. Now secure the pins vertically with the points either up or down.

❖ Hold the pieces right sides together, and insert a pin through a right-hand corner point (or left if you are left-handed), again checking this by flipping the pieces over. Now bring the pin up along the sewing line on both sides of the pieces. Place another pin so that it enters the fabric 1.25cm (½in) from the end and comes up through the corner.

Assembling a Block

Whether you are making a block you have designed yourself, or are following written instructions, you should have a clear idea of the piecing sequence you should follow. It is helpful to pin your pieces onto a polystyrene board (four ceiling tiles stuck to a piece of board is excellent for this). As you finish piecing each unit, pin it back into place on the board, so you can see the progress. This tip can be particularly helpful in some blocks where there can be thirty-six pieces, or more!

Hand Stitching

To piece by hand, use running stitches with an occasional backstitch (about every 2cm/¾in) to add strength. Use a plain thread, cotton is best, and a 'sharp' needle. Cut about 45cm (18in) of thread and tie a knot in the end. Hold your pinned pieces firmly

in one hand and remove the first pin. Insert the needle from the back, 3mm (⅛in) from the corner along the marked line, and take a backstitch to the corner, flipping as you go to make sure your stitches are on the line. Sew along the line, always flipping until you are confident the stitch line is straight, taking the odd backstitch and removing the pins as you go. At the end, do another backstitch, but insert the needle through the loop as you form the last stitch. Sew the pieces for a block into the units shown in the instructions, then press these units.

Pressing

When pressing patchwork it is important to be gentle; you don't want to distort the pieces. Unlike dressmaking, when you press the seams open, in patchwork you press the seam to one side, usually towards the darker fabric. In this way, the seams are stronger and less visible on the right side. Once the units are pressed, you can go on and sew the rows.

Finger pressing This is useful when you are sewing short seams, particularly in hand piecing. Simply press the seam to one side or the other with your fingers and thumbs. (Once again, press towards the darker fabric so that the shadow will not show under the lighter one.) You can also use a ruler to press by running the flat edge down the seam.

Pressing completed blocks Pressing can make a great difference to the accuracy of completed patchwork. If you iron too aggressively, you could stretch the fabrics and cause distortion. Lower the iron onto the back of your patchwork and move gently over the seams. When you have pressed the wrong side of your patchwork, iron the right side, preferably in one direction.

Joining Rows

To join patchwork rows, first hold the pieces right sides together and insert a pin at the exact point where the seams and corners meet. Pin all such places along the row, then pin through the marked seam lines between the corner pins. Sew together with running stitch and the occasional backstitch as before. At each seam put the needle through the seam allowances and make a backstitch on the other side. The seam allowances should not be sewn down. Once finished, press the completed rows.

MACHINE PIECING

Machine piecing is a valid part of the craft of patchwork today whatever the purists may say. For quilts that are going to take a lot of wear and tear or that have to be made in a hurry, you cannot beat machine piecing. Follow the rules below to make the whole process quicker and easier, since there is nothing quite as dispiriting as unpicking machine stitches!

Get to know your sewing machine Study the manual and see what special devices and tricks it has. Practise on spare fabric and learn to control the machine 'automatically' so you don't have to worry about your foot. Make sure it is cleaned and oiled regularly, particularly before and after a heavy sewing session.

Prepare for work Make sure you are comfortable. Wind plenty of bobbins in a neutral or complementary colour before you start, so you don't have to keep stopping. It is important also to make a practice block before you start a marathon piecing session to check that you have got it right. Press this block, then measure it to be sure it is coming up to the size it should.

Seam allowances Machine piecing *always* requires a 0.5cm (¼in) seam allowance, and it is well worth checking to see if your machine has a foot that is exactly this width. If your machine has no such foot, and you can't buy one, then place a guide on the throat plate of the machine. To do this, mark an accurate 0.5cm (¼in) from the edge of a piece of paper. Without threading the machine, sew along the 0.5cm (¼in) line until you have about 7cm (3in) either side of the foot (see Fig.3). Stick a piece of masking tape along the edge of the paper to become a guide. If you wish, you can stick several more layers

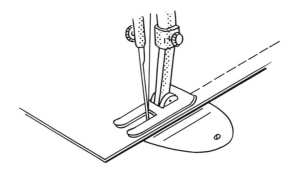

FIG 3

on top to form a ridge against which the fabric can slide.

Cut accurately You do not need to mark the sewing line for machine piecing, but it is important that cutting is accurate. Make sure that templates include the 0.5cm (¼in) seam allowance – all the templates for machine piecing in this book do. If you are planning to use any of those given for machine piecing, you will find it helpful to cut off the points of the templates to within 0.5cm (¼in) of your seam line, see Fig.4.

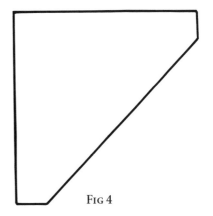

FIG 4

Note the straight grain When placing your templates on fabric for cutting, take a careful note of the straight grain. This is marked with a long arrow on the templates given in this book. The line on the template should run parallel with the edge of the fabric, so the pieces are cut on the straight (firm) grain rather than the bias (stretchy).

Cutting To cut your patches, first make a template (see page 17). Place the template onto your fabric and mark the outline in pencil. Alternatively, you can place the template under a rotary ruler and cut along the ruler with a rotary cutter (see page 16). In this way you can cut out several layers at once.

Plan ahead Always plan the piecing order of each block carefully. Many of the blocks in this book have an exploded diagram by them showing the order in which they should be sewn by number. *Always* piece a sample block first – this will get you used to the order in which it should be pieced, and when it is finished, you can measure it to be sure that it turns out the right size. For example, when sewn, a 30cm (12in) block should measure 32cm (12½in) including the seam allowances.

Machine sewing Put the first two pieces to sew right sides together, and place them under the machine foot. Lower the needle by hand, rotating the wheel at the right of the machine until the needle is firmly in the fabric. This will lock the stitch so the needle will not unthread and the first few stitches are

less likely to disappear in a bunch down the hole in the throat plate.

If you are sewing lots of pairs of fabrics together at once, it is easier to chain piece several at a time. Start the first seam as described above and sew to the end of the seam, but *don't* lift the needle from the fabric. Get your next pair ready and insert them under the machine foot and start stitching again (see Fig.5). You will form a couple of stitches in thin air before the next seam but you can go on adding pair after pair this way. Continue until they are all sewn, then cut them apart. Press with the seams towards the darker fabric wherever possible. Repeat this with all the units in turn.

Once the units are pressed, lay them out in the correct order and start sewing them into larger units. For example, for a Ninepatch block, three rows of three, sew the top, then the middle, then the botton row, finally sewing the three rows together.

When machine sewing units together, pin them first and try to make the seam allowances face in opposite directions (see Fig.6). This will make them fit together more easily and will also help make the seams flatter.

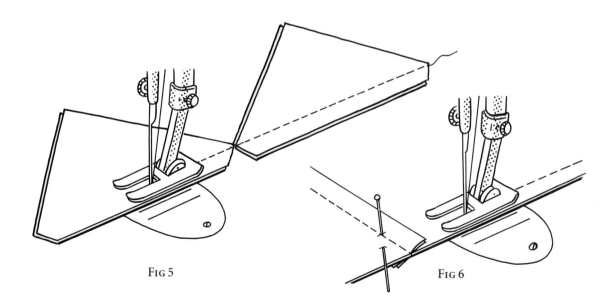

Fig 5

Fig 6

HAND QUILTING

Quilting is formed by two fabrics with a layer of padding between them, being sewn together with lines of simple straight stitching, or beautiful and complex designs, such as those found in many of the traditional English quilts. Quilted clothes are light and warm and in recent years have come back into fashion. As a result of this, quilting is popular again because it can be used in so many practical or purely decorative ways.

THE QUILTING PROCESS

The quilting process begins with preparations for quilting, including marking out a design, tacking up or sandwiching the quilt layers, followed by the actual quilting. If you are intending to quilt a patchwork project you may wish to 'outline' quilt it, in which case omit the next stage, except for any areas (usually plain fabric areas) where you plan a more elaborate design.

Marking Out a Design

See page 16 for advice on enlarging and tracing the quilting pattern. Press your top fabric layer well and lay it on a flat surface ready to mark out your quilting design using one of the following methods.

❧ The easiest method is to tape your design to a light box, well-lit window or glass-topped table with a lamp underneath it. The light will show through even dark fabrics. Using masking tape, tape your fabric on top of the design and then mark the design with pencil or water-erasable marker.

❧ Use coloured pencils (dark for light fabrics and light for dark fabrics) to draw around your template or use a ruler for straight lines. You can also use a water-erasable marker for this.

Tacking Up

Before tacking up, make sure both your top and backing layers are well pressed as it will not be possible to do it after quilting. However, do *not* iron

your fabric after marking with a water-erasable marker as the marks sometimes 'set' with heat.

To tack up, or make a quilt 'sandwich', first place the backing fabric right side down on a flat surface (the floor if it's a quilt), then add the wadding (well smoothed out) then finally the top fabric with the right side uppermost. Tack the layers together from the top. Don't lift the layers too much as you tack, as it will pull them out of position. Work from the middle towards the edges, forming a grid pattern (see Fig.7). It is important to tack the layers together firmly to prevent them shifting as you quilt, especially if you do not intend to use a frame or hoop.

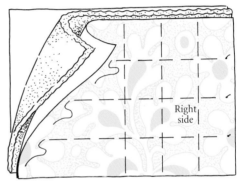

FIG 7

If you are using a hoop or frame, place the work into it after tacking up. With a frame pin it in with lots of safety pins. If using a hoop, place it in the centre of your quilt and fasten it fairly tightly, but leave a bit of 'give'.

Quilting

The quilting stitch is an evenly spaced running stitch which should appear the same on both sides of the work. It is more important that the stitches are even than small, and you will soon find your own 'tension'.

Start the sewing in the centre of the work and quilt outwards. Always use a single strand of thread. If used double, the strands will rub together, making them weaker not stronger. The length of thread depends on its strength and/or the ease of sewing.

Work with one hand underneath the quilt to feel the needle coming down and to help it back up again. It saves 'finger-wear' if you can get used to wearing a thimble or guard on this hand as well! The sewing hand controls the needle from the top side of the work. Make each running stitch in one movement, not a stab stitch, except where the thickness of seams makes quilting difficult. With practice it is possible

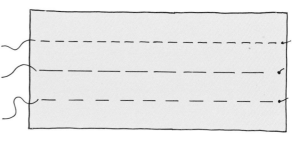

FIG 8

TYPES OF HAND QUILTING

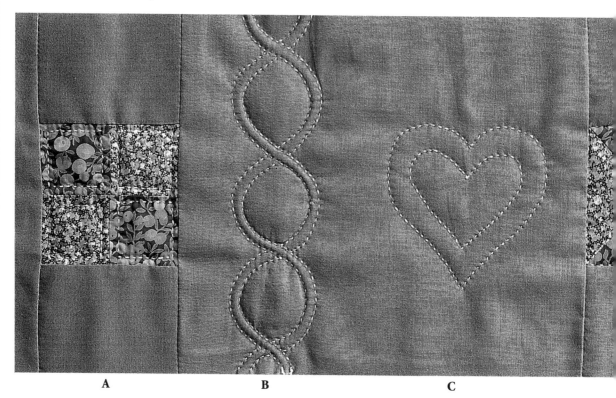

A	B	C

A *Outline quilting* This is often used with patchwork, especially if the pieced work is intricate. The quilting is worked approximately 0.5cm (¼in) away from the patchwork seams, holding the layers together and enhancing the patchwork effect.

B *Italian or corded quilting* This is a technique where lengths of soft wool or yarn are threaded from the back of the fabric through channels

formed by lines of stitching to give a raised or corded effect.

C *English or wadded quilting* This is the elaborate quilting seen in Durham and Welsh quilts, usually worked in toning thread on plain fabric.

D *Quilting 'in the ditch'* This type of quilting can also be done by machine and is used to complement a patchwork design when extra lines

to take more than one stitch at a time and to develop a rhythm. By practising the quilting stitch you will be able to vary the stitch length to one you feel comfortable with. The evenness of the stitching is more important than the size (see Fig 8, page 22).

Sometimes the seam allowance can be a nuisance, showing through to the front and making it much harder to quilt. Using a long, straw needle,

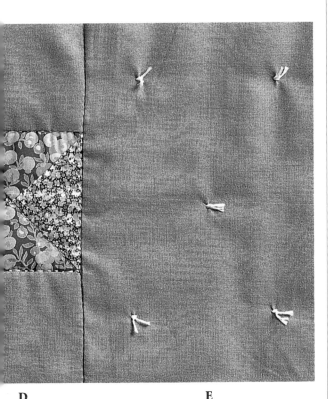

D   **E**

of stitching are not desired but the quilt layers still need to be held together. The stitching is done with a toning thread in the seam line where the pieces have been joined.

E *Tying* If working on a thickly padded item such as a cot quilt, it is often easier to hold the layers together by tying. The knots are formed about 15cm (6in) apart, by taking a stitch and making a reef knot (see page 34).

MAKING A QUILTER'S KNOT

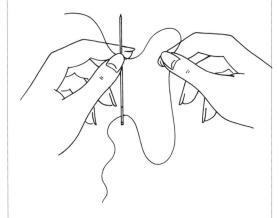

Fig. 9a Thread the needle and lay the long 'tail' of thread across the needle.

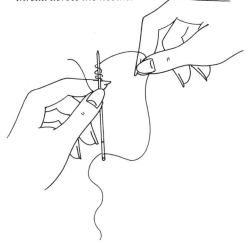

Fig. 9b Wrap the 'tail' of thread loosely around the needle several times.

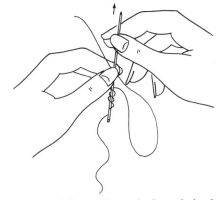

Fig. 9c Pull the needle gently through the thread and a flat knot will be formed.

*Sashiko Tied Cushion
(see page 116)*

slide it between the top fabric and the seam allowances, parallel to the seam, and use to smooth the seam allowances back under the pieced area.

To begin a thread Make a 'quilter's knot' (see Figs.9a, b and c on page 23) and insert the needle about 1.25cm (½in) from the start of the design and bring it up at the start. Give a slight, sharp tug and the knot will pop between the layers to lose itself in the wadding.

To fasten off After the last stitch take a small backstitch through the wadding and top only. Pierce this backstitch with the point of the needle (to anchor it) and run the thread off into the wadding before snipping off the thread.

MACHINE QUILTING

As with machine piecing, machine quilting is a perfectly valid technique which, being very quick compared to quilting by hand, will save a great deal of time. Wonderful decorative effects can be achieved using the vast range of metallic, shiny and multicoloured threads available today. Decorative machine stitches can also be used for quilting – consult your sewing machine manual. There are also some very good books on machine quilting available at libraries. It can be daunting to even try quilting by machine however, because if anything goes wrong it

will take hours to unpick. It is therefore *essential* that you practise on spare fabric first until you are confident. Having said that, it is not that difficult if you follow certain rules.

❧ Tack your layers together thoroughly to help prevent too much shifting about of the layers. Before you start, make sure you are comfortable and if necessary raise the sewing machine to enable you to sit squarely with your shoulders straight.

❧ Use a medium-length machine stitch (about twelve). To work straight lines, close to patchwork seam lines for example, use the usual machine tension.

❧ If you wish to quilt freehand, curved motifs for example, drop the feed dogs on the machine and guide the piece through the machine with your hands. A hoop to hold the tension for you can be helpful. Most sewing machine manuals will explain what to do for that machine.

❧ Try to work fairly quickly as that seems to be more successful than slow, painstaking progress. Work from one side of your piece to the other, and roll the bulk to enable it to fit under the machine foot.

❖ Finish at the edges wherever possible to reduce the number of thread ends you will need to deal with. Cut the threads at the edges and the ends will be caught in the binding or finishing. When fastening ends in the centre however, pull both threads to the wrong side, make a knot, then thread the two ends onto a needle and lose the ends in the wadding.

APPLIQUÉ

Appliqué involves laying and attaching one piece of fabric over another to create a decorative design. There are many applications, from a child's pinafore to tea-cosies and full-size quilts, and there are several methods, outlined below.

Buttonhole Stitch Appliqué

Here, buttonhole stitch is used around the edges of an appliqué motif to enhance the design and cover raw edges (therefore no seam allowances are needed). It is easier to do when the motif is attached to the backing using fusible web. Buttonhole stitch (see page 29) is most effective on projects which will need washing and those needing extra colour.

Over Papers Appliqué

In this type of appliqué the appliqué motif is traced onto paper, with no seam allowances. The fabric is then cut, allowing for a 0.5cm (¼in) seam allowance. Place the paper on the wrong side of the fabric and pull the seam allowance over towards the paper, clipping corners and curves where necessary. Tack the fabric all round then sew to the background fabric using tiny hemming stitches. Remove the tacking. With sharp, pointed scissors, split the background fabric behind the appliqué and take out the paper. To finish, slipstitch the split closed. This method is appropriate for fine and complicated designs such as quilts and delicate clothing.

Interfaced Appliqué (Fusible Webbing Appliqué)

For this method you need soft, non-iron interfacing.

Trace your motif onto the interfacing and cut it out leaving approximately 2.5cm (1in) all round. Cut out the fabric to the same size. Place the interfacing on top of the right side of the fabric and sew all round the marked line by hand or machine, leaving no gaps. Trim the seam allowance to approximately 3mm (⅛in). Make a split in the centre of the interfacing and turn the fabric through the split. Use a knitting needle point to smooth the seam, then press your motif. It is now ready to stitch to your background fabric with small hemming stitches.

This is an easier and more durable form of hand appliqué and is appropriate for reasonably fine work which you want to do quickly. If you prefer this appliqué can also be machined into place using a decorative stitch or invisible machine hemming.

Machine Appliqué

When you attach an appliqué motif with machine stitching you get a durable finish, ideal for items that will be washed frequently, such as children's clothes. Satin stitch, which is quite narrow and close, is the best stitch to use, and its shiny effect will enhance the appliqué. Iron your motif in place with fusible webbing and it will be held firm ready to stitch.

Stitch and Tear Templates

These are used mainly in appliqué to help make it as accurate as possible. Each different shape in a block has a template. Using the template, you cut out the relevant number of pieces and sew them together to make up an accurate block.

BINDING

Binding, with either straight or bias strips, is by far the most popular way to finish a piece of patchwork, particularly if it is quilted. The binding goes around the edges of the quilt sandwich and encases all the layers. Usually the first fold (see Fig.10a, page 26) is sewn into place by machine, then the binding is pulled over to the back (see Fig.10b) and hemstitched into place.

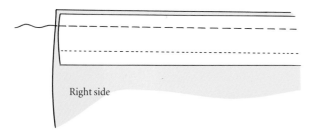

Right side

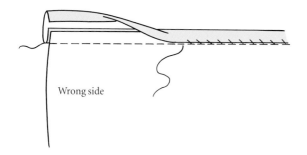

Wrong side

FIG 10a & b

FIG 11

Using Bias Binding

This is more flexible and will leave a smoother finish, especially on curves. It is available commercially or you can make your own – see below.

Binding with Straight Strips

These are ideal if you want to bind the quilt with one of the fabrics used in the quilt. Cut four strips approximately 20cm (8in) longer than the length of the quilt and 4cm (1½in) wide, and sew it into place as you would the bias binding shown above.

Using Double Edging

If you are making a quilt which will have lots of use, it is advisable to use double-fold binding. Because there is a double thickness, it will not wear out as quickly. Cut the binding 6.5cm (2½in) wide, fold it in half lengthways, apply the raw edge to the quilt edge as shown in Fig.11, then hemstitch the folded edge into place on the back of the quilt, in the same way as single binding, shown in Fig 10b (above).

Making Bias Binding

This is most essential when you can't find the colour to finish a project. It is rather hit-or-miss in terms of

quantity however: a lot of binding can be made from a modest amount of fabric. If you wish, you can buy a bias making tool, with which you can iron your binding and automatically produce a hem fold at each edge. This is worth investing in if you prefer to have a hem pressed for you.

To make about 9m (9¾yd) of binding follow the steps in Figs.13a–e on page 27.

FINISHING CORNERS

To finish corners neatly, place one border over the other. Then, using a pencil and ruler, draw a line from the quilt corner to the overlap corner (see Fig.12). Swap the uppermost corner and draw the same line. Using the lines as sewing guides, pin and sew from innermost to the outer corner. Trim away the seam allowance, leaving 0.5cm (¼in) then press.

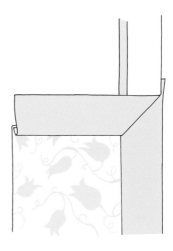

FIG 12

MAKING BIAS BINDING

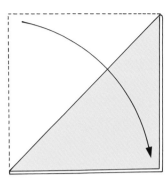

Fig.13a *Fold a 60cm (24in) square of fabric in half diagonally then cut along the fold to produce two triangles. Sew the edges together taking a 0.5cm (¼in) seam allowance.*

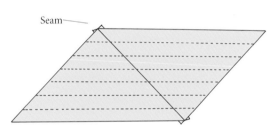

Fig.13b *Press open to give the rhombus shape shown. Mark lines 4cm (1½in) apart across the fabric.*

Fig.13c *With right sides together, sew crosswise edges together offsetting the marked lines by one bias width and so producing a 'tube' of fabric.*

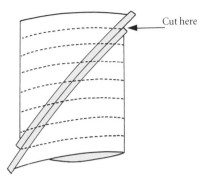

Fig.13d *Beginning at the extended edge, cut along the marked lines.*

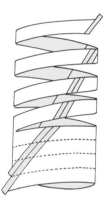

Fig.13e *Cutting along the marked lines produces a long continuous strip.*

Bias binding edging on the London Stairs Quilt (page 31)

EMBROIDERING AND SIGNING WORK

Embroidery works well with patchwork, quilting and appliqué. It can be used to enhance details of flowers, animals, birds and so on, or to embellish the finished patchwork or appliqué. Some hand embroidery stitches used in this book, are shown under Stitches in this section, but refer to a book of embroidery stitches for further inspiration.

Machine embroidery may be used to equally great effect as hand embroidery. Most modern sewing machines have at least a limited range of embroidery stitches built in, and the computer models have amazing ranges to choose from. Machine embroidery stitches can be used as quilting because the machine stitches are strong enough to hold the quilt sandwich together. Try a decorative machine stitch as a change from a straight one next time you are machine quilting a project.

Every piece of work you do is for a purpose, whether for your own use or as a gift or fund raiser. It is important therefore to take the time to mark your work with your name, the date, who it is for and perhaps why. It will always be interesting for you, for it is surprising how quickly you forget when you made a particular item. Those for whom you made it would also appreciate the documentation and of course there is the thought that in years to come future owners will also wish to know the origins of their heirloom!

STITCH SAMPLER

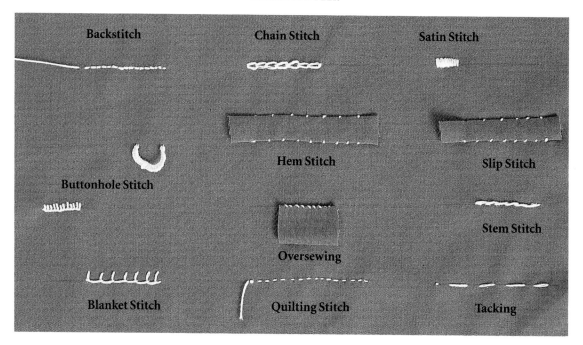

This stitch sampler shows all the stitches you will need to make the projects in this book.

STITCHES

Backstitch

This is a linear stitch which appears as a continuous line of small stitches. Bring the needle up through the front of the fabric at 1, down at 2 (which should be next to the last stitch) and up at 3.

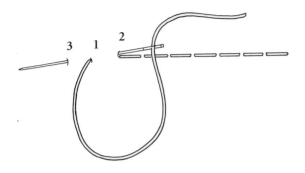

Blanket Stitch

This is a very variable and useful stitch which can be worked with different densities of stitches and with varying stitch lengths. Bring the thread out on the lower line shown in the diagram. Re-insert the needle at 1 on the upper line and out again at 2, with the thread under the needle point so that a loop is formed.

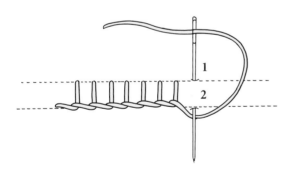

Buttonhole Stitch

This is done in the same way as blanket stitch (above) but the stitches are knotted and placed closer together.

Chain Stitch

Chain stitch is very useful for creating patterns and textures or simply when a row of stitches is required. Bring the needle out to the front of the fabric and insert it at 1. Bring it out again at 2, with the thread looped under the point of the needle. Continue to work the next stitch by inserting the needle at 2 and out as before, and so on.

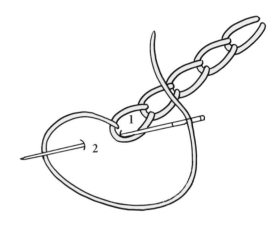

Hem Stitch

Make a small vertical stitch to start, going from 1 to 3 as shown on the diagram. Bring the needle out at 1, in at 2, out at 3 and back in at 4. Bring the needle down horizontally to start another stitch.

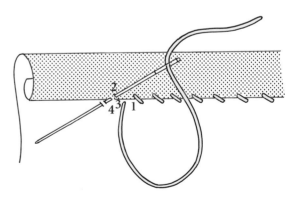

Oversewing

This is a method of attaching two pieces of fabric together, commonly used in hand piecing for patchwork. Simply take small stitches through both layers of the fabric, working along the line to be stitched.

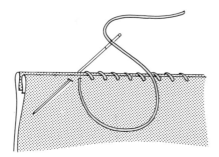

Quilting Stitch

The quilting stitch is basically a small, neat running stitch, with the thread being passed under and over the fabric. Bring the needle out to the front of the fabric at 1 and insert it at 2. Bring the needle out at 3 and repeat.

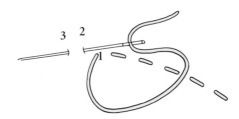

Satin Stitch

This is a long, smooth stitch which covers the fabric well and is a good filling-in stitch. Straight stitches (see below) are worked closely together across the shape to be embroidered, with care taken to maintain

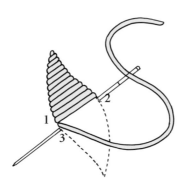

a neat edge. Avoid making the stitches too long. Bring the needle out to the front of the fabric at 1. Insert it at 2 and then bring out again at 3, and so on.

Stem Stitch

This stitch is used for outlines, flower stems and so on, and can be used as a filling stitch. Work from left to right, taking small, regular stitches along the line of the design. The thread should always emerge on the left side of the previous stitch. Bring the needle out to the front of the fabric at 1. Insert it at 2 and bring out again at 3, and so on.

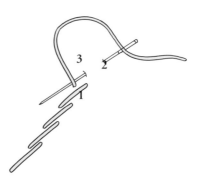

Straight Stitch

This stitch can be worked either regularly or irregularly. The stitches can be of varying sizes but should not be too long or loose. Bring the needle out to the front of the fabric at 1. Insert it at 2 and out again at 3, and so on.

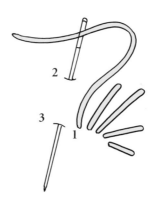

London Stairs Quilts

London Stairs is a very old, traditional patchwork design which is very simple to make, though the finished effect can look deceptively complicated. It makes an ideal first project. I have used the design to create a baby's quilt, with a scaled-down version for a doll's quilt. If you create a different design from the one shown in the photograph, you may have to alter the fabric requirements accordingly.

Finished size: baby's quilt 138×76cm (54½×30in); doll's quilt 47×36cm (18½×14in)

FOR THE BABY'S QUILT YOU WILL NEED

Four fabrics, each 0.5m (½yd) by 112cm (44in) wide

Border fabric (select one of the fabrics in the quilt), 0.75m (¾yd) by 112cm (44in) wide

2oz wadding, 127×96.5cm (50×38in)

Backing fabric, 1.5m (1½yd) by 112cm (44in) wide

Purchased or home-made bias binding, 5m (5yd)

Thread to match

Basic sewing kit and a sewing machine if desired

FOR THE DOLL'S QUILT YOU WILL NEED

Four fabrics, each 0.25m (¼yd) by 112cm (44in) wide

Border fabric (select one of the fabrics in the quilt), 0.25m (¼yd) by 112cm (44in) wide

2oz wadding, 43×33cm (17×13in)

Backing fabric, 43×33cm (17×13in)

Purchased or home-made bias binding, 2m (2yd)

Thread to match

Basic sewing kit and a sewing machine if desired

To Make the Quilts

Both the baby and doll's quilts are made in the same way until it comes to the quilting, then separate instructions are given for this.

Note: The seam allowance rule for hand/machine piecing is relevant here (see box on page 17).

1 First wash, dry and iron your fabrics. Using template A (if making the baby quilt) or template B (if making the doll's quilt), cut out twenty-four blue, twenty-four red, twenty-four green and twenty-four yellow pieces of fabric. (If using a rotary cutter see page 16.) Lay the fabric pieces in four separate piles according to colour. Numbering the fabrics at this stage will help you when stitching the blocks together.

2 Cut out the border fabric as follows. For the baby's quilt cut four side borders 67×9cm (26×3½in), (these will be joined in the middle), and two top and bottom borders 112×9cm (44×3½in).

For the doll's quilt cut two side borders 47×4cm (18½×1½in) and two top and bottom borders 32×4cm (12½×1½in) wide.

3 Referring to the photograph on page 34, take the first two pieces and sew them together by hand or machine (see hand piecing, page 17 or machine piecing, page 19). This will make one unit. Repeat with all the pairs on the top row.

4 Press the seams towards the darker fabrics on all units (see pressing, page 18). Join the units together to form the top row, checking constantly against the photograph on page 34 (see joining rows, page 18). Press the seams flat. Repeat steps 3 and 4 for all the other strips.

5 Lay all the strips in place on the floor to be sure they are in the right order, and then sew them together. Press thoroughly.

6 Take two side border strips and sew them together to form one long strip then do the same with the other pair. Carefully pin a border piece along one long side of the quilt. Taking a 0.5cm (¼in) seam allowance, sew into place, then repeat on the other side. (Putting the pins in sideways will allow you to sew over them and thus save tacking.)

7 Trim the ends of the borders flush with the end of the quilt. Pin and sew the top and bottom borders into place across the borders and sew. Press the seams to the darker fabrics.

Quilting the Baby's Quilt

8 First, mark the quilt top (see quilting process, page 21). Using the piecing and quilting pattern as a guide, take a sharp silver or white pencil and a ruler and mark the quilting lines on to the quilt top (see marking out a design, page 21).

9 Make a template of the curved shape on page 35 and cut out (see making templates, page 17). Use this template to mark the quilting design on to the border as shown in the piecing and quilting pattern.

10 Now sandwich the quilt layers (see tacking up, page 21). Press your backing fabric carefully and lay it right side down on a table or floor. Spread the wadding on top of the backing fabric, making sure it is central before smoothing it out. Place the quilt top right side up over the wadding, and, working from the centre, smooth it out. Pin or tack the three layers together.

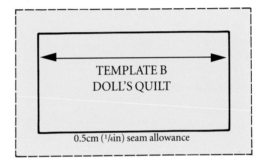

TEMPLATE B
DOLL'S QUILT

0.5cm (¼in) seam allowance

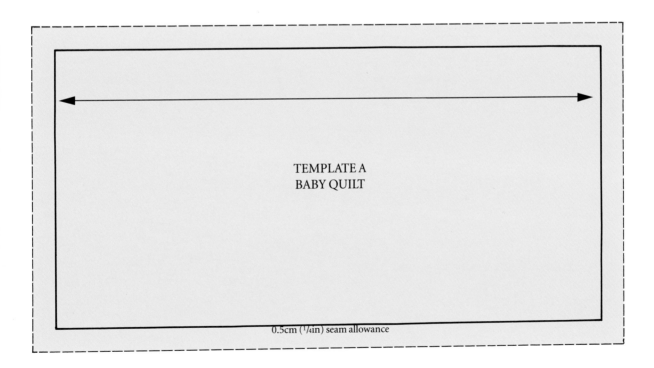

TEMPLATE A
BABY QUILT

0.5cm (¼in) seam allowance

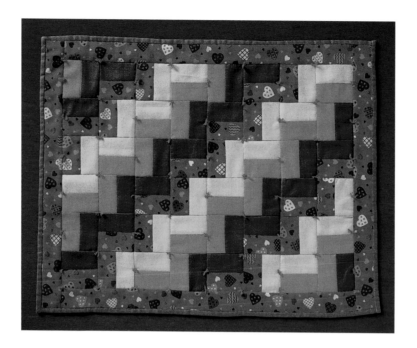

11 To complete the quilting, follow the instructions for quilting on page 21, quilting along all the marked lines on the quilt top.

12 To finish the baby's quilt follow the instructions for binding a quilt on page 25.

Quilting the Doll's Quilt

The layers in this project are tied rather than quilted together. If you are working on a thickly padded item such as a cot quilt, it is usually easier to hold the layers together by tying. The ties or knots are formed by taking a stitch (using a thick thread such as button thread, crochet cotton or knitting wool) and making a reef knot which won't come undone. Place the knots in lines approximately 15cm (6in) apart, or use the patchwork as a guide. The knots can be left on the front or reverse side.

13 Sandwich the three layers together as described in step 10. Using reef knots (see Fig.1), tie through all three layers at the points shown in the photograph.

14 Bind the quilt as before, following the instructions for binding on page 25.

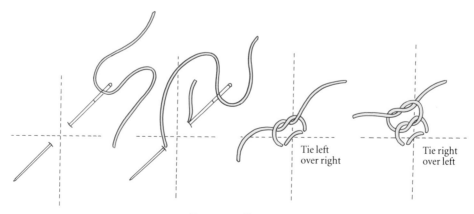

Tie left over right

Tie right over left

FIG 1 *Reef knot*

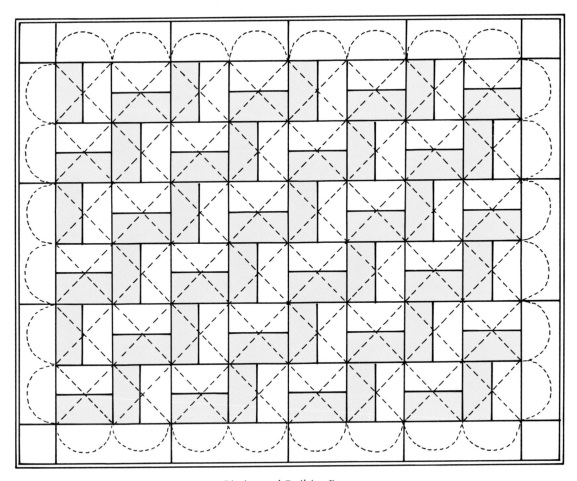

Piecing and Quilting Pattern

BABY QUILT BORDER TEMPLATE

'Mood Indigo' Shoulder Bag

*This shoulder bag was made using soft denim from an old skirt and a
selection of indigo-dyed fabrics. I added the cutlery fabric for a bit of fun. The
choice of colours is up to you, so why not spend some time experimenting?
This bag is quite easy to make if you follow the instructions carefully, and it
will become a useful addition to your accessories.*

This bag uses a technique called foundation piecing,
as does the Christmas Stocking on page 61. This
technique involves stitching patchwork layers, by
hand or machine, to a background fabric. The
resulting pieced section can be used as you wish. For
example, you could turn a seam allowance under
and appliqué the design into place as the main
component of a piece of work, or sew it together
with other pieced designs.

Finished size: 28×33cm (11×13in)

YOU WILL NEED

Backing fabric (unbleached calico or old sheeting),
    71×30cm (28×12in)
2oz wadding, 71×30cm (28×12in)
Lining fabric (select from one of the patchwork
    fabrics or cotton chambray), 71×30cm (28×12in)
Denim, 1½m (1½yd) of 90cm (36in) wide (or long
    lengths such as legs of old jeans)
Scraps of indigo-blue fabrics
Navy blue thread
One wooden toggle
Safety pins

1 Mark out your backing fabric following the
measurements shown in Fig.1. To do this first
fold the fabric in half widthways and either crease
the fold line well or run a line of temporary tacking
stitches across it.

2 From the fold line measure 7.5cm (3in) above
it and mark a line in ball-point pen right across
the fabric width (see Fig.1). This is line A. Do the
same below the fold line to draw another line, B.
Now measure 7.5cm (3in) from the top of the fabric
piece and draw line C. Measure the same amount at
the bottom of the fabric and draw line D. Finally,
measure 5cm (2in) in from each side of the backing
fabric piece and draw in lines C and D.

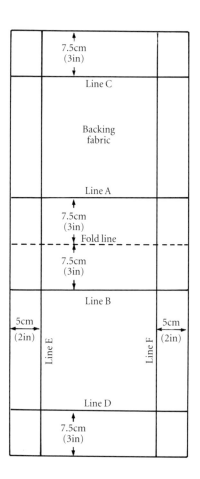

FIG 1

36

3 Lay the lining fabric out flat, right side down on a table or floor. Lay the piece of wadding on top and smooth out. Lay the marked backing fabric on top of the wadding, right side up and smooth out again. Safety pin the three layers together in a sandwich.

4 From the indigo-blue fabrics cut strips measuring about 7.5×28cm (3×11in) ready to begin the foundation piecing.

Foundation Piecing (steps 5–6)

5 Place the first indigo fabric strip at an angle along line A, making sure it just covers the line (see Fig.2). Sew in place. Place a second indigo fabric strip, right sides together with the first. Pin and sew together 0.5cm (¼in) from the raw edges along one long side and anchoring the pieces to the backing fabric. Lift the second fabric strip and finger press the seam open. Add a third strip of fabric, right sides together with the second strip but at a slightly different angle (see photograph, page 37), and

repeat the sewing and finger pressing. Continue to join the strips together in this way until the top half of the backing fabric is covered to above line C.

6 Repeat step 5 to cover the bottom half of the backing fabric from line B to line D. You should end up with two pieced squares with a strip of uncovered backing fabric between them.

7 Cut a piece of denim 18×30cm (7×12in) and press a 1.25cm (½in) seam along each long side. Lay this in place on the strip of uncovered backing fabric, over the central fold line and the edges of the pieced squares (see Fig.3). Pin in place, then topstitch about 3mm (⅛in) from the edge on both sides.

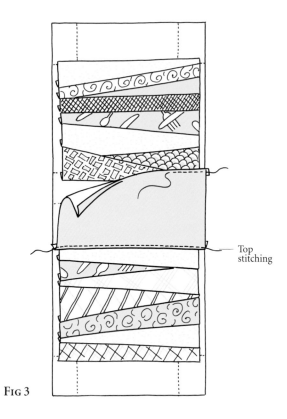

Fig 3

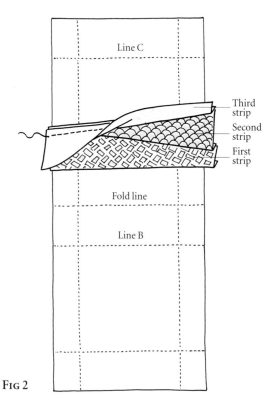

Line C

Third strip

Second strip

First strip

Fold line

Line B

Fig 2

8 Cut two strips of denim 6×74cm (2½×29in) and lay them along either side of the pieced squares on lines E and F, right sides together. Tack into place then press open (see Fig.4, page 39).

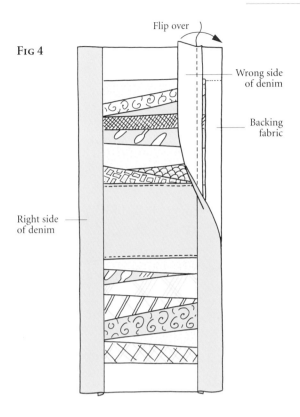

FIG 4

Flip over

Wrong side of denim

Backing fabric

Right side of denim

9 Cut two pieces of denim 18×30cm (7×12in) and sew a 1.25cm (½in) hem along one long side of each piece. Sew the denim pieces with right sides together to each end of the pieced foundation block allowing for a 1.25cm (½in) seam allowance and leaving a 2.5cm (1in) gap along one side only (as shown in Fig.5). Press open. The ends of these top facings will be longer than the foundation piece but they will fold down later to become hems.

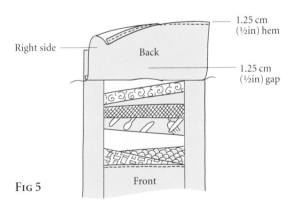

Right side

Back

1.25 cm (½in) hem

1.25 cm (½in) gap

Front

FIG 5

10 Fold the pieced material in half, right sides together and, leaving a 1.25cm (½in) gap about 2.5cm (1in) from the top of each side, sew the side seams together. It is as well to go over the seams two or three times to add strength. Trim the seams slightly then machine zigzag stitch to neaten. Turn to the right side.

11 Cut one length of denim 5×35.5cm (2×14in). Fold the strip right sides together lengthways, then pin and stitch, leaving a 1.25cm (½in) seam. Trim the seam back to about 3mm (⅛in) then turn the fabric tube through and press.

12 Cut three lengths of denim 117×5cm (46×2in) and make three tubes, as in the step above.

13 Take the three longest fabric tubes and pin and sew them together at one end, going over the seam several times. Plait the three strands firmly, then stitch them together at the other end.

14 Take the shorter tube and cut two 5cm (2in) pieces from it. Fold one piece over one end of the plait and stitch it in place. Repeat at the other end. Insert the raw edges into the gaps left in the side seams of the bag and stitch them firmly into place.

15 Fold the remaining length of tubing in half and oversew the last 10cm (4in) together (see Fig.6). Insert the raw edges into the 2.5cm (1in) gap left in step 9 and stitch firmly into place on the wrong side. Fold the edges of the top facings over to the wrong side and hemstitch into place.

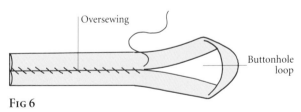

Oversewing

Buttonhole loop

FIG 6

16 Slipstitch the button loop onto the facing up to the fold and finally stitch the toggle firmly into place. Remove tacking stitches.

Pinwheel Tissue Box Cover

Tidy up your dressing table with this stylish tissue box cover. It is designed to cover a square box, and the colours have been chosen to match a teenager's bedroom. The block used is an 8cm (3in) Pinwheel.

Finished size: 13cm (5in) high by 12cm (4¾in) wide

YOU WILL NEED

One square 'boutique' tissue box

Two toning, plain fabrics each 0.25m (¼yd)
Patterned fabric 0.5m (½yd)
Wadding scraps
Small quantity of plain, toning fabric for binding
Thread to match

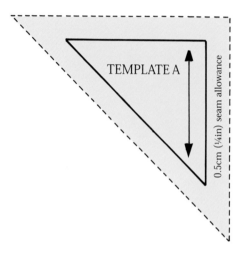

TEMPLATE A

0.5cm (¼in) seam allowance

1 Cut twenty pieces of each plain coloured fabric using template A. Then following the piecing number order shown in Fig.1, piece four Pinwheel blocks. Press carefully (see pressing, page 18). Lay the other block pieces aside for the moment.

these pieces with the four blocks made above in one long line so: strip + block + strip + block + strip +

2 From the patterned fabric cut a strip 4.5×34cm (1¾×13½in). Cut into four widthways and join

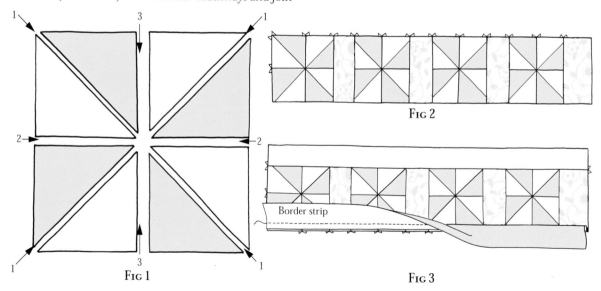

FIG 1

FIG 2

Border strip

FIG 3

4 Cut a strip of patterned fabric and a strip of wadding 44.5×18cm (17½×7in). Lay the patterned fabric right side down, place the wadding and finally the pieced strip right side up on top. Pin together and sew down the raw edges. Place the short ends together and machine stitch taking a 0.5cm (¼in) seam allowance to make the main cover 'tube'. Trim the seam then zigzag stitch to neaten.

5 To make the 'lid', piece the final Pinwheel block in two halves but do *not* join together. Now cut strips of scrap patterned fabric 4cm (1½in) wide and stitch to three sides of the Pinwheel halves. Press carefully and trim the edges flush.

6 Cut two pieces of wadding and patterned fabric the same sizes as the pieced blocks. Layer them as follows: wadding, pieced block right sides up, then patterned fabric right side down.

7 Stitch along the non-bordered edge of the pieced halves taking a 0.5cm (¼in) seam allowance (Fig.4). Trim the seam allowance, then flip the patterned fabric back over the wadding to create a lining and pin the three layers together (see Fig.5). Repeat with the other half block. Place these two right sides together and oversew (see Fig.5).

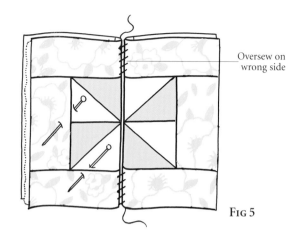

Oversew on wrong side

FIG 5

8 Place the resulting square on top of the main cover 'tube' and, matching the centre seams of the side and top blocks, pin together.

9 Using the other plain fabric, cut four strips 15cm (6in) by 2.5cm (1in) wide. With wrong sides together, pin this binding into place along the top edge of the cover (see Fig.6) and taking a 0.5cm (¼in) seam allowance, stitch into place. Repeat on the other side, then turning a hem as you stitch, slipstitch the binding into place. Do the same on the other two sides, taking care to catch in the ends of the binding neatly.

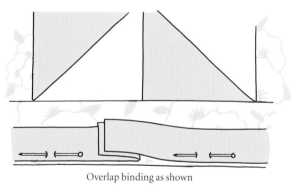

Overlap binding as shown

FIG 6

10 To bind the bottom edge cut a strip of fabric 2.5cm (1in) wide by 46cm (18in) long. Stitch this right sides together with the bottom edge of the cover, overlapping the ends. Turn to the wrong side and slipstitch the hem. To finish, put the cover on the tissue box.

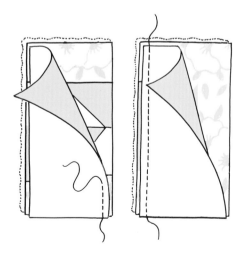

FIG 4

Quilter's Jewel

Here is a charming idea that is useful for any needleperson but which works particularly well for quilters, since they do so much hand sewing. The domed centre is a pincushion, with eight reels of quilting thread strung around the edges. The idea is based on a Victorian pincushion, and I was delighted to include this design in a book of gifts to make published by Oxfam in 1992 for their 50th Anniversary. It would be useful made in colours to match a room and you could easily make several for yourself and quilting friends.

Finished size: 20cm (8in) diameter

YOU WILL NEED

Two fat quarters of co-ordinating fabrics,
    preferably 100% cotton

Stuffing (eg, old tights, lamb's wool, polyester
    wadding or bran)

Thin card (eg, birthday cards or postcards)

Medium-thickness card (eg, cereal packets)

Thick card

Threads for sewing, in matching colours

Glue (UHU or Copydex)

Toning ribbon, 1m (1yd) of 1.25cm (½in) wide

Awl or paper punch

1 From thin card cut one template A (see page 45) and eight template B. From medium card cut eight template C. From thick card cut one template D.

2 Cut fabric for each piece allowing a 0.5cm (¼in) seam allowance. Tack the fabric pieces around pieces A and B in preparation for English piecing (see page 16), but glue templates C and D to the wrong side of the cut fabric pieces, overlapping the seam allowances onto the card.

3 Oversew pieces A and B together on the wrong side (see Fig.1). Bend the C pieces at the lines

shown on template C using a ruler to fold against. Oversew the eight C pieces into place around the A and B pieces, and then oversew around the points of pieces C to complete the top (Fig.2).

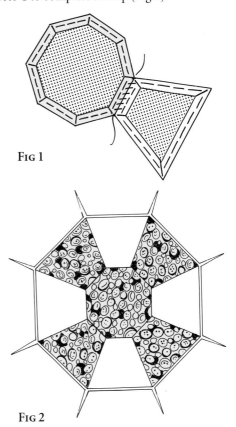

FIG 1

FIG 2

4 Remove the card from the A and B pieces, but *not* the C pieces. Now oversew six edges of piece D (the base) onto the completed top on the

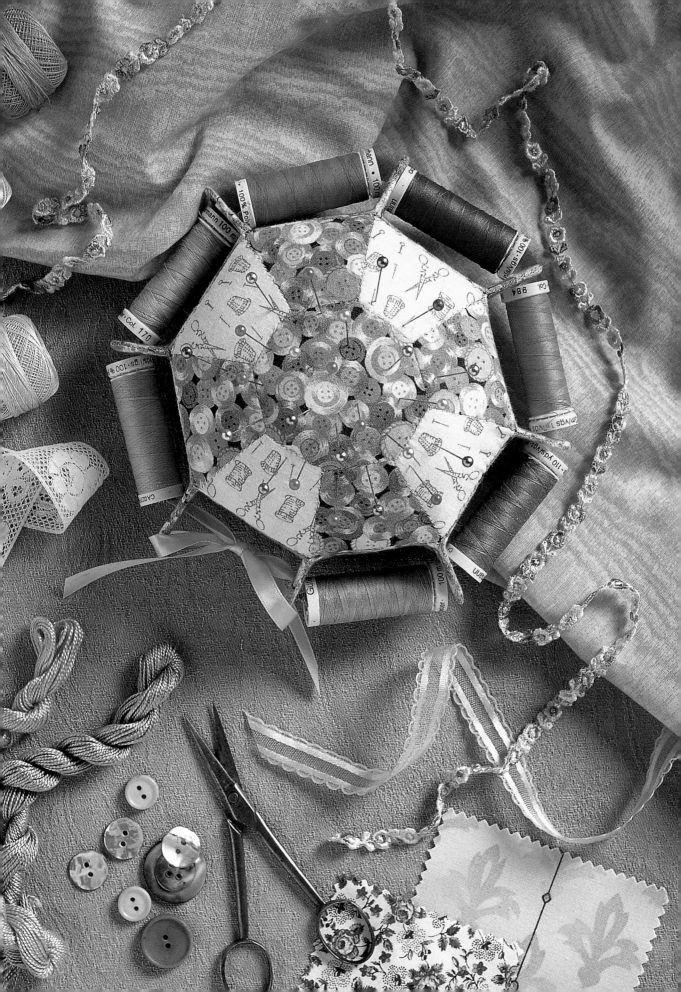

outside (see Fig.3), and then stuff firmly before stitching the two final seams.

5 Using an awl or paper punch, make holes on the points as shown on template C. Thread the ribbon through the first hole, through a reel of cotton, then through the second hole and so on. Cut the ribbon ends into points and finish with a bow.

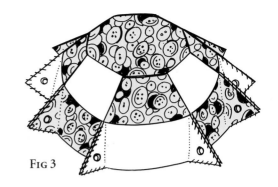

FIG 3

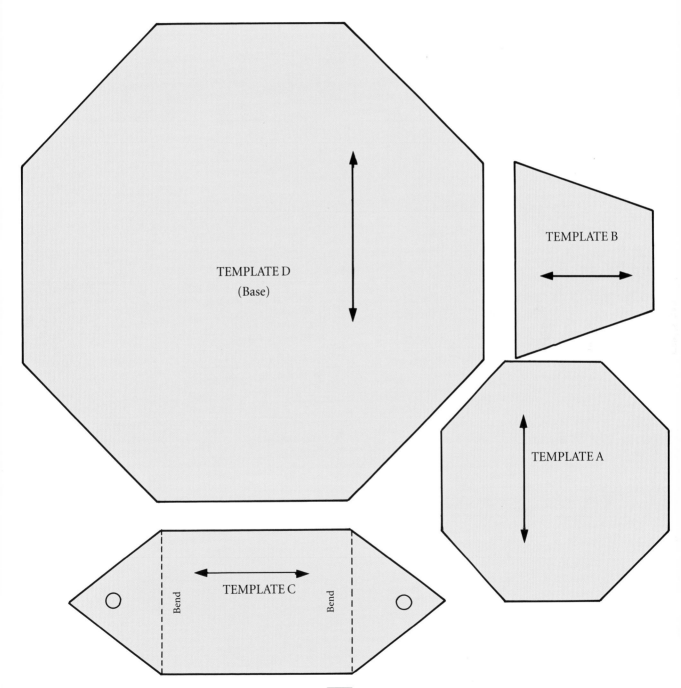

TEMPLATE D
(Base)

TEMPLATE B

TEMPLATE A

TEMPLATE C

Bend

Bend

Pot of Gold Wall Hanging

Suffolk Puff or Yo-Yo is an odd patchwork technique. It is usually made without a backing when used for a quilt, which must leave plenty of places to catch your toes! It is also time consuming, though each little puff can be made quite quickly and it is a useful project to carry around. It is ideal for decorative pieces such as the trees in the Country Scene Neck Purse or a badge in the Spring Basket Wall Hanging. This colourful design developed from a packet of twelve rainbow colours dyed by a company in Alaska. I wanted to make a colourful statement with them and this was the result.

Finished size (with frame): 58.5cm (23in) square

YOU WILL NEED

Graded selection of twelve rainbow-coloured fabrics (or pack CW01 from Alaska Dyeworks – see Suppliers page 126)

Black 100% cotton fabric, 2m (2¼yd) by 152cm (60in) wide

Gold beads, 2mm wide (about 325)

Black thread

Piece of corrugated cardboard, about 60cm (24in) square

Mount board, two squares 58.5cm (23in) and one square 57cm (22½in)

2oz wadding, two pieces 58.5cm (23in) square

Glue (eg Copydex)

Two curtain rings

1 Cut twelve 7cm (2¾in) diameter circles in each of the rainbow fabrics. You will probably find it best to make a template (see page 17).

2 Turn a 0.5cm (¼in) hem around each circle and starting with a knot, sew around the edge with doubled black thread. Gather the stitches tightly and fasten off using two or three stitches. Flatten the stitches in the centre of the puff and pinch the fabric, teasing it into a circular shape.

3 Once all the puffs are done, pin them in order onto a piece of corrugated cardboard, following the colour order in the photograph.

4 Using double thread, sew the puffs together as follows. Knot the thread then slide the needle in through the centre of the puff and out at one side (see Fig.1). Take one or two small stitches to anchor the thread. Thread a bead on to the needle and catch a small stitch on the side of another puff. Come back through the bead to the first puff and take another small stitch. Repeat this two or three times and fasten off. With the next puff, use the bead as a guide to keep the rows straight. A long needle helps here. Sew the puffs into rows, then join the rows.

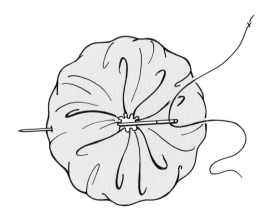

FIG 1

5 Take one of the 58.5cm (23in) square pieces of mount board and measure 8cm (3in) from the outer edge at several points, marking with a pencil. Join the marks to make a 42cm (16½in) inner square. Cut this square out.

6 Cover this mount board frame with one piece of the wadding, glue into place, then trim the wadding out of the aperture.

7 Cut a piece of black fabric 68.5cm (27in) square and iron it. Place the fabric right side down on a firm surface and centre the wadded frame on top, wadding side down. Pull the fabric corners up and over and glue them down. Then glue the side edges, pulling as you go to create a tension. From the wrong side, trim a square from the centre of the black fabric, leaving 2cm (¾in) all round for turning and gluing. Snip almost into the corners to help the fabric stretch, and pull the edges through the aperture to the back of the frame and glue them down. Leave the frame overnight to dry thoroughly.

8 Place the frame right side up on a table and sew in the puffs as you sewed them together, again using gold beads. You will find it easier to sew in the four corners and the centre puffs on each side to create a tension first.

9 Cover the other 58.5cm (23in) square of mount board in wadding and black fabric in the same way as before. Glue the frame right side up to the other covered board, sandwiching the puffed patchwork between them. Pinch together with clothes pegs or bulldog clips and leave to dry.

10 Glue the last piece of mount board to the back of the hanging, covering the raw edges. Stitch on the two curtain rings, one at each side of the hanging.

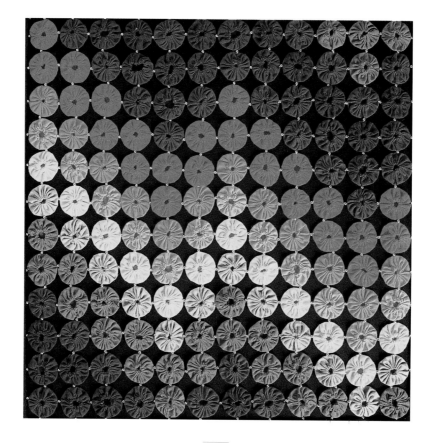

Spring Basket Wall Hanging

This project will bring a hint of spring to your room, no matter what time of year it may be! The simple patchwork basket block could be used for a cushion or a quilt; simply make as many blocks as you need, sew them together with flowered fabric sashing and you have a fresh spring look. This basket contains flower badges in pretty pastels which you can wear or leave in the basket as an ever-fresh arrangement. You could also use the hanging to store your favourite badges and brooches.

Finished size: 43cm (17in) square

YOU WILL NEED

Plain, dark green fabric, 0.25m (¼yd)

Pale green fabric, 0.5m (½yd)

Yellow-patterned fabric, 0.25m (¼yd)

Flower-patterned fabric, 0.5m (½yd)

Matching thread for sewing and quilting

2oz wadding, 0.25m (¼yd)

Backing fabric, 0.5m (½yd)

Bias binding, bought or home-made

For the flower badges:

Scraps of pastel-coloured fabrics

Small cardboard squares

Matching thread

Brooch bars or safety pins

Glue (eg Copydex)

1 From the template patterns A, B and C provided on page 52, make your templates for the lower half of the basket and the handle (see making and using templates, page 17).

2 Begin the hand piecing by marking and cutting your fabric pieces (see page 17) as follows (making sure you follow the fabric grain line).
Cut six template A in dark green fabric.
Cut five template A in yellow-patterned fabric.
Cut one template B and one BR in pale green fabric.

Cut one template C in yellow-patterned fabric. Also cut a piece of pale green fabric 16.5×32cm (6½× 12½in) for the upper part of the basket.

3 Following the piecing pattern on page 50, hand piece the lower half of the block (see hand piecing, page 17). Now hand appliqué the handle into place on the plain upper half of the block (see over papers appliqué, page 25).

4 Place the upper and lower halves of the block right sides together and, taking a 0.5cm (¼in) seam allowance sew the two halves together.

5 Cut 9cm (3½in) wide border strips in floral fabric and sew these around the block, mitring the corners as you go (see page 26).

6 Create a quilt sandwich with the backing, wadding and top (see tacking up, page 21) and then quilt (see quilting, page 21). You can create your own design or follow the quilting pattern on page 50.

7 Bind your hanging (see binding, page 25), and sew a sleeve at the back. To make a sleeve, take a strip of fabric about 25cm (10in) wide and 10cm (4in) less than the quilt width. Turn a narrow hem at each end. Fold in half lengthways, right sides together and sew to make a tube. Turn the sleeve to the right side and slipstitch the top and bottom of its length to the back of the quilt near the top, leaving a tube through which to thread a pole.

To Make the Flower Badges

8 For the hexagon-shaped flower, make a rosette in pastel fabrics as described on page 67.

9 For the Yo-Yo flower, cut seven 5cm (2in) circles and gather them as described in the Pot of Gold Wall Hanging on page 46.

10 For the gathered petal flower, cut five 10cm (4in) squares of floral fabric. Fold one in half, then half again, creating a smaller square. Using double thread and a strong knot, make a length of running stitch from corner to corner through the layers. Gather up this stitch, which will bunch up the fabric, then fasten off securely. Create the other four 'petals' from the remaining fabric squares, then oversew them together to create a flower. Place a button or yo-yo or whatever you like in the middle.

11 Once you have created your 'flowers', glue a cardboard square (about 2.5cm/1in) onto the back. When this is dry, glue the brooch bar or safety pin into place. Arrange the flowers as you wish in your basket.

Piecing and Quilting Pattern

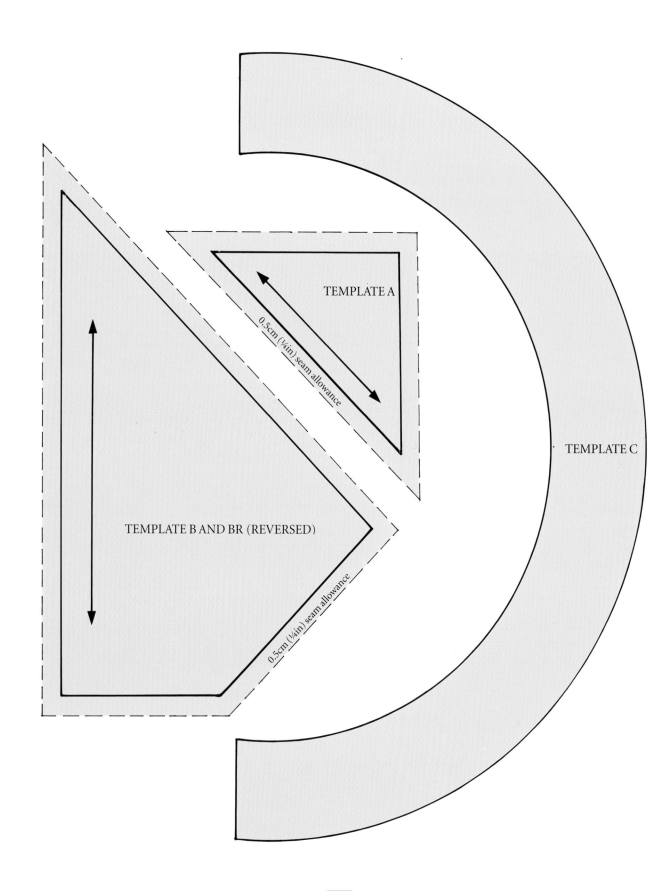

TEMPLATE A

TEMPLATE C

0.5cm (¼in) seam allowance

TEMPLATE B AND BR (REVERSED)

0.5cm (¼in) seam allowance

Liberty Hearts Quilt

Patchwork and appliqué are often seen together in old quilts and the effect can be very charming. This project, using Liberty scraps, was made much easier with the use of interfaced appliqué. I learned this technique in a mini workshop in Houston, Texas 1989 from a lady called Jean V. Johnson. Thank you Jean, appliqué has since become a pleasure to me. The full instructions for interfaced appliqué will be found on page 25 in the Basic Techniques section.

Finished size: 131cm (51½in) square

YOU WILL NEED

Plain, white fabric (for background), 1m (1yd)

Scraps of fabrics, none less than 4cm (1⅝in) wide and 29cm (11½in) long, and containing a selection of larger scraps for the appliqué hearts

Fabric (for borders), 0.25m (¼yd) by 114cm (45in) wide

Soft, non-iron interfacing (for appliqué), 0.75m (¾yd)

2oz wadding, 140cm (55in) square

White backing fabric, 140cm (55in) square (this *must* be white or it will show through the white squares at the front and spoil the look of the quilt)

White sewing thread

White quilting thread

1 First wash, dry and iron your fabrics. Then proceed to make the larger striped squares as follows. Using a rotary cutter or scissors, cut a quantity of 6.5cm (2.5in) wide strips in blue and mainly blue fabrics. Cut sixteen 19cm (7½in) squares of paper – old photocopies will do. You will be sewing onto paper which makes it easier to sew straight seams and helps to make the fabric (especially lawn) more stable.

2 Fold a strip of fabric in half lengthways, place the fold line on two diagonally opposite corners of a square and pin. Place the next strip right sides together with the first and sew down one edge taking a 0.5cm (¼in) seam allowance and sewing through the paper as well.

3 Finger press the seam open and place the next strip right sides together on the right-hand edge and repeat until one half is covered with fabric. Turn the square upside down and repeat until the other side is covered. Do the same with all squares.

4 With the paper side facing you, trim around all the blocks to the paper. Now slide the blade of your scissors carefully up a paper channel (see Fig.1). Be careful to only cut the paper *not* the fabric. Fold the cut paper edge on the right hand seam and tear off the paper at the sewing line perforations. Remove all the paper this way.

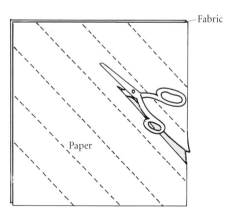

FIG 1

5 Cut forty-eight 9cm (3½in) squares of paper and make striped squares in the same way as before using 4cm (1½in) strips of fabric (colours as before) which will be 2.5cm (1in) wide when sewn. Trim and remove the paper as with the larger squares.

6 Make the heart squares by first cutting twenty 19cm (7½in) squares from your fabric scraps and sixteen 9cm (3½in) squares from the white fabric. Next cut twenty hearts in pink-patterned fabric using template A on page 57 and sew diagonally onto the background squares using interfaced appliqué (see page 25). Then cut sixteen pink-patterned hearts using template B and appliqué these to the smaller squares.

7 Using the piecing and quilting pattern on page 56 as a guide, piece together all the larger squares. From the border fabric cut four strips 114×5cm (45×2in) and sew them around the centre section of the quilt taking a 0.5cm (¼in) seam allowance and mitring the corners (see page 26). For the border, piece and add the smaller squares as shown in the piecing and quilting pattern.

8 Quilt your wall hanging as shown in the piecing and quilting pattern on page 56 (see quilting, page 21).

9 Finally, bind your quilt (see binding, page 25). I used commercial bias binding, but if you prefer you can use all the scraps joined widthways as straight binding.

Piecing and Quilting Pattern

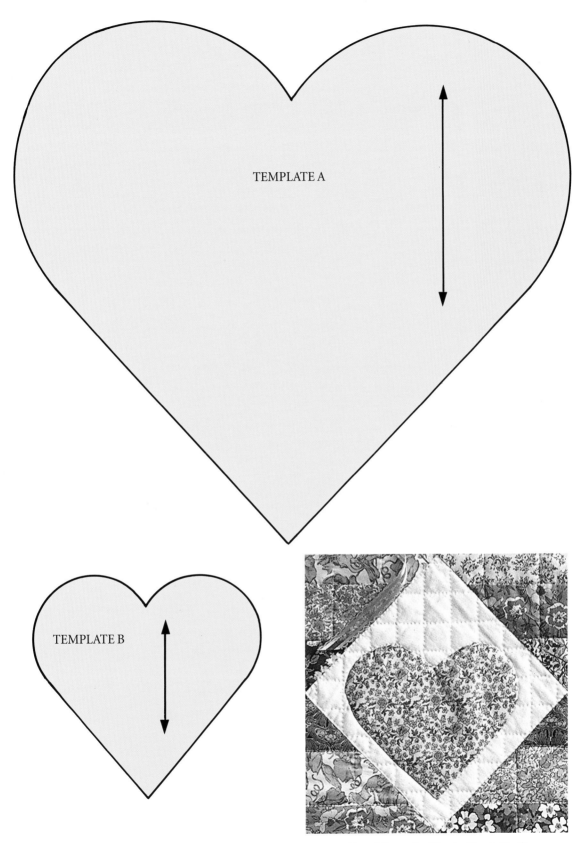

TEMPLATE A

TEMPLATE B

Detail from the Liberty Hearts Quilt

Puffed Cot Quilt

This design is very popular, especially with the youngsters, though few can resist squeezing the puffs! Although designed primarily as a cot quilt, this item can also be used as a floor play mat, in the playpen or in the car.

Finished size: 74×92cm (29×36in)

YOU WILL NEED

Cotton backing fabric, 1m (1yd) by 112cm (44in) wide

Four cotton fabrics (I used blue, mint, yellow and pink), each 0.5m (½yd) by 112cm (44in) wide

2oz wadding (flame resistant), 1m (1yd) by 128cm (50in) wide

Polyester toy stuffing (flame resistant) for puffs (amount varies depending on how firmly you stuff the puffs)

Plain white cotton fabric, 1.25m (1¼yd) to back the puffs

White thread

Rainbow embroidery silk for tying

1 First wash, dry and iron your fabrics. If you wish to hand cut the squares with scissors, make the templates in card or plastic (see page 17). Template A is an 11.5cm (4½in) square, and template B is a 14cm (5½in) square. If you use a rotary cutter, use your ruler to measure the strip width you need to cut the squares.

2 Cut sixty-three template A squares in white fabric for the back of the puffs. Cut sixteen template B squares in each of the mint, yellow, pink and blue fabrics (one will be 'spare' or over).

3 With wrong sides together, and with the right side facing you, match a coloured square with a white one. Line up the top left-hand corners and

pin them together. Line up the right-hand corners and pin. This will leave spare fabric in the middle. Fold this to the right to make a pleat. Repeat on two more sides. On the fourth side, pin the pleat in the coloured fabric, but *not* through the white.

4 Machine or hand sew around the four sides (see Fig.1), taking a 0.5cm (¼in) seam allowance, and leaving the fourth side partially open. Repeat with all the other squares.

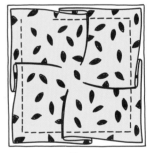

FIG 1

5 Take a handful of stuffing and stuff it into the square through the open side. Make sure you get into the corners but stuff sparingly – you do not want it to be too firm. Tack the opening closed. *Safety Note:* Be careful that the resulting quilt is not too heavy – it can be very dangerous for small babies to get too hot.

6 Using the photograph on page 59 as a guide, lay the squares out in rows. Take the first two puffs in a row, place them right sides together and taking a 0.5cm (¼in) seam allowance, sew them together. Lay them back in order and add the next

puff. Continue until the row is finished, then stitch all the other rows. Join the rows together in the same way (Fig.2).

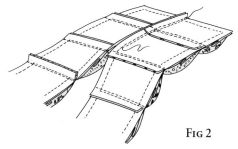

FIG 3

FIG 2

Pin through all layers, and taking a 0.5cm (¼in) seam allowance, sew around the puffed top by hand or machine. Tie the three layers together where four corners meet on the quilt (see Fig.3 and page 34).

7 Press the backing fabric and lay it right side down on a flat surface. Place the wadding on top and the pieced puffs on top of that. Trim the wadding to 4cm (1½in) all round the puffed piece.

8 Trim the backing fabric so that it is 4cm (1½in) bigger all round than the wadding. Turn and press a 0.5cm (¼in) hem round all four sides. Pin into place next to the puffs. Hemstitch into place.

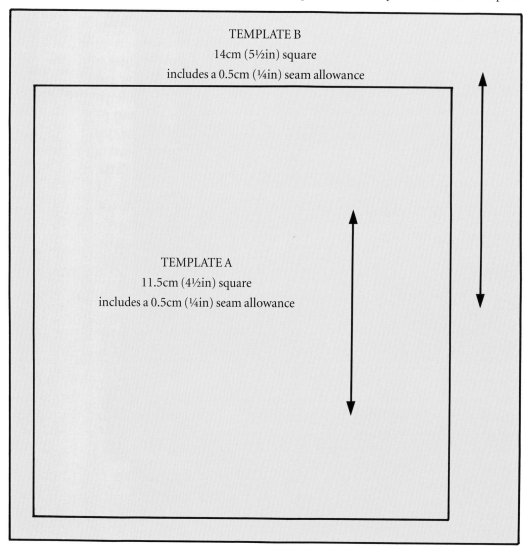

TEMPLATE B
14cm (5½in) square
includes a 0.5cm (¼in) seam allowance

TEMPLATE A
11.5cm (4½in) square
includes a 0.5cm (¼in) seam allowance

Christmas Tree Decorations

Christmas is a lovely time for making patchwork decorations – you can use lots of glittering metallic fabrics, or shades of the more traditional red and green. Here are three different patchwork tree decorations for you to try – I leave the colour choices to you!

TREE STOCKING

This stocking is designed to hold small presents – perhaps sweetmeats, trinkets or handmade toys. Larger versions of the stocking can be made by enlarging the pattern by 200% for a 34cm (13½in) size and 400% for a 68cm (27in) size.

Finished size: 17cm (6¾in) long

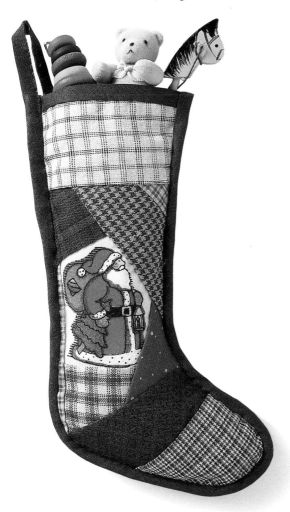

YOU WILL NEED

Scraps of Christmas fabrics, including small motifs
Small quantity of plain fabric (for the lining and background fabric)
Bias binding to tone
Thread to tone
Buttons and beads (optional)

To Make the Foundation Piece
Foundation piecing involves stitching patchwork layers to a background fabric and was also used in the 'Mood Indigo' Shoulder Bag on page 36.

1 First, draw your stocking outline onto the plain fabric leaving a large area around it. Place a motif or scrap of Christmas fabric onto the plain fabric foundation stocking piece (see Fig. 1), and pin

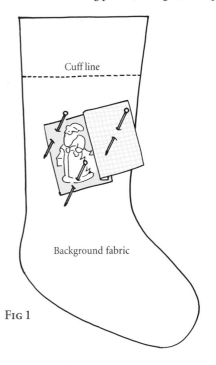

Cuff line

Background fabric

Fig 1

into place. Place a strip of fabric right sides together with the first piece and pin into place. Then taking a 0.5cm (¼in) seam allowance, sew into place. Finger press the seam open and pin the new layer down.

2 Place the next strip right sides together with one of the previous strips. Stitch, taking a 0.5cm (¼in) seam allowance and finger press the seam open. Repeat this procedure to the marked cuff line making sure you go slightly beyond it, then work the other way towards the toe of the stocking covering all the foundation.

To Make the Stocking

3 For the lining, fold a piece of plain fabric in half right sides together. Place the stocking template on the fabric, draw around it and cut out. Set aside.

4 Place the stocking template back on top of the foundation piece, draw around it and, leaving a 0.5cm (¼in) seam allowance, cut out the shape.

Cuff line

STOCKING TEMPLATE

Right A pretty tree for Christmas, decorated with the Tree Stocking, the Amish-Style Tree Decoration, the Hexagon Rosette and the Country-Style Tree Skirt (see page 68)

5 Cut a straight 'cuff' piece for the front of the stocking and one stocking piece (reversed) for the stocking back in white, green or red fabric.

6 Sew the 'cuff' to the front of the stocking, right sides together, either by hand or by machine taking a 0.5cm (¼in) seam allowance as shown in Fig.2.

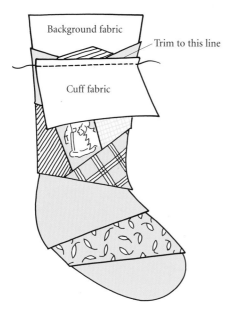

Fig 2

7 Pin the pieced stocking front to one of the lining pieces, wrong sides together. Tack all around the edge, then trim back to the edge of the foundation piece. Pin the stocking back to the second lining piece, again with wrong sides together, and tack to keep in place.

8 Bind the top edge of each half of the stocking, making sure that you have included the lining fabric too. Place the two halves of the stocking together, with the linings facing each other. Pin, then bind (see page 25) all around the edge, leaving 10cm (4in) of binding free at the stocking top diagonally opposite the toe. Next, hemstitch the binding into place, and when you get to the free edge, turn the end in neatly and oversew down to make a hanging loop. Add any buttons, beads or other ornamentation you wish.

9 Finally, fill the stocking with goodies! You may want to include toys permanently, as shown in the photograph on page 63. If you do, fill most of the stocking with scraps of wadding or tissues, then glue or stitch the toys firmly into place at the top.

AMISH-STYLE TREE DECORATION

This simple block design is one of many you could choose to make using foundation piecing.

Finished size: 9cm (3½in) square

YOU WILL NEED

Scraps of Christmas fabrics including some with motifs (one must be big enough to cover the back of the pieced block)

Square of plain, white or cream fabric at least 10cm (4in)

Masking tape

Safety pin

Matching thread

Bought or home-made bias binding

1 First trace the Amish block template on the page opposite onto the plain fabric background square (see marking out a design, page 21). (It may help if you trace the design onto paper first using a permanent felt-tip pen.) Using masking tape to secure, stick the background fabric uppermost on the paper tracing and trace the design onto the fabric with a pencil.

2 Decide which fabrics you are going to place where and begin by cutting a piece of fabric with a motif on it larger than the centre square. Lay it face up on the wrong side of the background fabric. Hold the square up to the light to be sure the central square is covered and that the motif is central. Pin into place with a safety pin (this is useful as it will help to stop the thread catching on an ordinary pin).

3 Take a piece of the next fabric chosen and lay it right sides together with the centre square (see Fig.1). Stitch it by hand or machine from the wrong side through the three layers, taking a 0.5cm (¼in) seam allowance and using the drawn line as your sewing line. Open the seam and finger press it open, then pin it open.

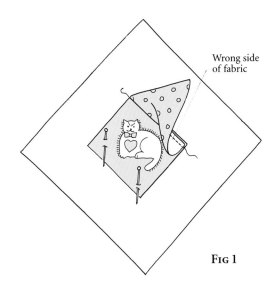

Wrong side of fabric

Fig 1

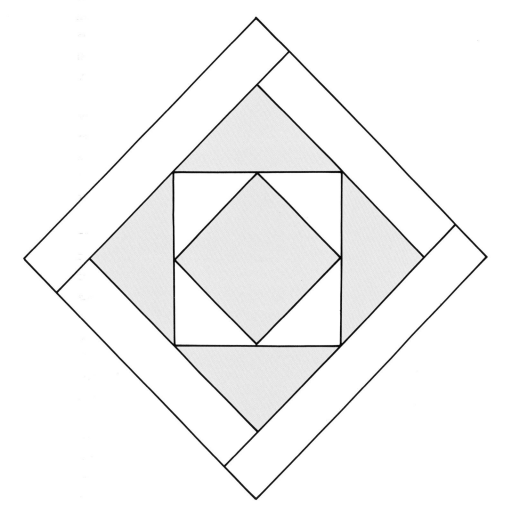

AMISH-STYLE DECORATION TEMPLATE

6 Bind the lower two sides of the block (see Fig.2, below). Pin the bias binding to the left-hand top edge, leaving a strip of binding about 7.5cm (3in) long, then pin down the right side (see Fig.3). Hemstitch the binding up one side, then, holding the folded bias binding together, oversew for 7.5cm (3in). Now finish hemming the binding into place and neaten the end as shown in the Christmas stocking project on page 64.

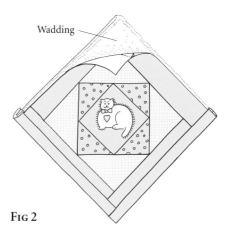

Wadding

FIG 2

4 Place the next piece on top of the next corner and sew into place. Repeat on the other two corners. Sew the next 'round' of fabrics into place in the same way.

5 Cut four strips of your final choice of fabric and sew them into place, finger pressing the seams open. Tack between the two outside lines of the square and then trim the piece to the outside line – this leaves you with a complete square. Cut a square of patterned fabric the same size as the trimmed block and pin it into place on the back of the block.

Note: The second line in is the sewing line. In this instance you will use it as a guide for bias binding, but if you wished to sew several blocks together, you would use it as the seam guide.

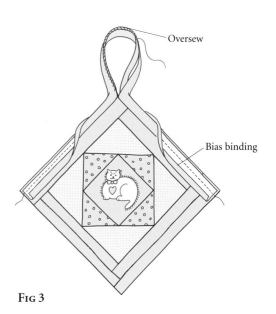

Oversew

Bias binding

FIG 3

7 Decorate the back of the block with buttons, sequins or other ornamentation.

HEXAGON ROSETTE TREE DECORATION

This dainty tree decoration is all the nicer for the cute little angel in the centre. Look out for Christmas fabrics with these motifs, they are useful for all sorts of things, from decorations to cards, and a little goes a long way. This decoration is quick and easy to make and would be an ideal sale item for a Christmas bazaar. If you wish, you can make it in floral fabrics and add pot-pourri or lavender to the wadding to make a fragrant sachet.

Finished size: 6.5cm (2½in)

YOU WILL NEED

Scraps of Christmas fabrics (some with motifs)
Scraps of wadding
Matching thread
Ribbon, 10cm (4in)

1 Trace the full hexagon template onto paper, stick it to card and cut it out. This template is then used to cut the fabric. If you want to use template plastic instead, mark the sewing solid line in black felt-tip pen and you will make an instant window template. You can use this to select your motifs from various fabrics. You will need to cut fourteen fabric hexagons in all.

2 Make another template to the inner *solid* line of the hexagon template. Cut fourteen paper hexagons using this template and then follow the directions for English piecing on page 16. Arrange the fabric-covered paper hexagons how you wish and oversew them together to make two rosettes of seven hexagons.

3 Remove the tacking from the centre hexagons, then with wrong sides together, start to oversew the two together, removing the papers as and when you can. When you have oversewn the hexagons as far as shown in Fig.1, stuff lightly with scraps of wadding.

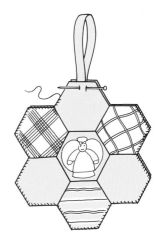

FIG 1

4 To make a loop, fold the piece of ribbon in half and place it between the seams as shown in Fig.1. Remove the final two papers and oversew the seams together, catching the ribbon into place.

Country-Style Tree Skirt

This is a good project with which to try freehand machine quilting. By using plaid fabrics and wooden beads as holly berries, you can create a primitive country feel to your tree skirt. We usually have a real tree which is thick at the bottom, so I have allowed a generous hole in the middle. I personally prefer just to cover the bucket, so this skirt isn't very deep. You will need to measure your requirements carefully before cutting your fabric.

Finished size: personal choice

YOU WILL NEED

Pale, checked background fabric, about 1.75m
    (1¾yd) of 152cm (60in) wide (curtain fabric may
    be a good choice)
Lining fabric, about 1.75m (1¾yd) of 152cm (60in)
    wide fabric (eg, plain sheeting)
Safety pins
2oz wadding, big enough to cover the skirt without
    a join
Assorted green plaid fabrics for the holly leaves
30 red buttons or beads (approximately) for the
    holly berries
Matching bought or home-made bias binding,
    about 5m (5yd)
Matching thread for machine embroidery and
    quilting
Bondaweb (for backing holly leaves)

1 First wash, dry and iron your fabrics. Lay the
background and lining on top of each other
and carefully fold into four (creating a smaller
square shape).

2 Mark the hole in the centre of the skirt by
placing a dinner plate (or something similar)
centrally on the folded corner of the fabrics and
draw an arc around the plate.

Drawing a Large Circle

3 To draw the outer circumference of the skirt
circle, first take a piece of paper (if you want to,
make a template first) or your fabric, approximately
7.5cm (3in) larger than the diameter you want. Fold
the paper or fabric into four and using a broom
handle or other long, straight object, draw the circle
in the following way. With someone else holding one
end of the pole at the centre fold, tape a ball-point
pen on the pole the required length from the centre
fold. With the end of the pole held in the central
position, carefully draw a curve along the quarter of

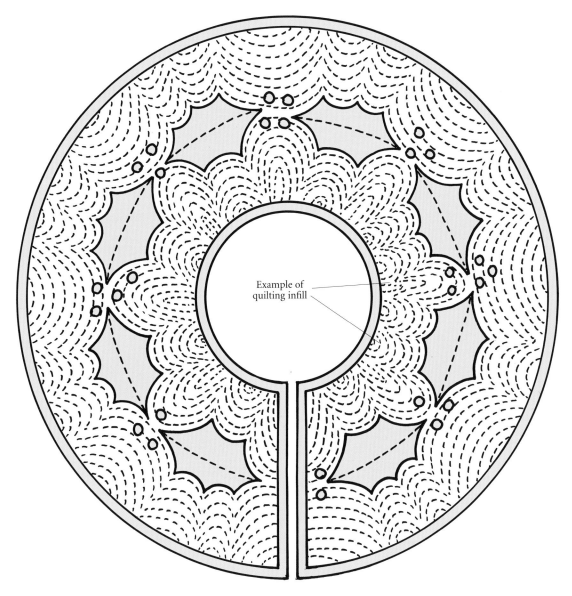

Example of
quilting infill

Appliqué and Quilting Pattern

the paper or fabric that is showing. Cut along the drawn line and you will have a circle when you unfold the paper or fabric.

4 Fold the fabric circle in half and make a straight cut from the outer circumference to the inner circle edge to make the opening.

5 Make a holly leaf template in card (see making templates, page 17) and draw around this eight

times onto the greaseproof paper side of the Bondaweb. Cut out the shapes. Iron the Bondaweb shapes on to the plaid fabrics and cut them out.

6 Decide where you want the leaves to go (see the pattern above for guidance), peel off the greaseproof and iron in place. Machine embroider around each leaf using a decorative or satin stitch. Sew a decorative stitch down each leaf centre.

7 Pin the backing, wadding and top fabrics together with safety pins. To machine quilt the skirt (see machine quilting, page 24) start with the first leaf at one end. Straight stitch a line 1cm (³/₈in) from the leaf edge, carry on to the next leaf and so on right across the skirt. Return to the beginning and sew the next line 1cm (³/₈in) from the first. Carry on this way until you reach the centre hole. In some areas you may need to infill a little but still try to keep 1cm (³/₈in) between each line. Turn the skirt around and start sewing from the other end in exactly the same way until you reach the outer edge, once again infilling as necessary.

8 Bind the edges of the opening, then around the centre hole, and finally the outer edge (see binding, page 25).

9 Sew the buttons into place where the holly leaves meet. Finally, fasten the skirt around the tree with safety pins, Velcro or perhaps with a button and loop.

Alternatively the tree skirt can be laid flat as in the photograph on page 63.

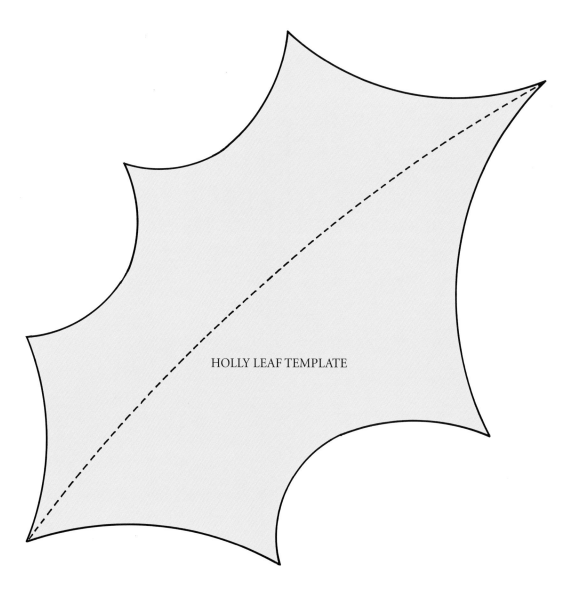

HOLLY LEAF TEMPLATE

Celtic Tea-Cosy

This type of design is known as Celtic because of the interlocking strands or knots which are so typical of the intricate artistry of the Celts. There are numerous stone crosses, jewellery artefacts and of course the Book of Kells, which provide inspiration for design. This tea-cosy has been made in a plain fabric and bound in a rich, patterned fabric which is overprinted with gold.

This pretty, delicate quilting technique is known as Italian quilting and can be used for collars and cuffs, and small items such as handkerchief sachets and ring cushions. It uses lengths of yarn or strands of soft wool, threaded from the back of the work through channels formed by lines of stitching, which gives a raised or corded effect.

Finished size: 40×27cm (15¾×10½in) (or of your choice)

YOU WILL NEED

Patterned fabric, 0.5m (½yd)
Plain fabric, 0.5m (½yd)
White fabric 0.5m (½yd)
Matching thread for sewing
Contrasting thread for quilting (I used a metallic thread)
Quilting wool, 2m (2yd)
2oz wadding, 0.5m (½yd)

1 Wash, dry and iron your fabrics. Enlarge the pattern on page 75 by 200% on a photocopier. Using the pattern, cut two patterned, two plain and two pieces of white fabric, leaving a generous seam allowance, and four pieces of wadding.

2 Trace the quilting design on to two of the plain fabric pieces, using a light-coloured pencil (see marking out a design, page 21). Make a sandwich with the plain fabric and the white fabric (see tacking up, page 21). You will not add the wadding until later. Repeat for the other side of the tea-cosy.

3 Quilt one side using the contrasting thread (see quilting, page 21). Metallic thread can snap easily so use short lengths to help prevent this. Repeat the quilting with the other side. As you can see the quilted design runs over and under itself, and it is important to follow this to create the right effect.

4 To stuff the quilting, thread a large tapestry needle with Italian quilting wool (a thicker, softer wool than the knitting variety, available from most quilt shops). Starting where a line goes 'under', push the wool through at the wrong side (see Fig.1). Pull the wool to the next corner or intersection and bring the needle out again on the wrong side. Leaving a loop of about 2cm (¾in) for ease, place the needle in again and repeat. Do this through all the channels. *Note:* If your channels are quite wide, you may need to use more than one strand of wool, and nestle them side by side in the channel.

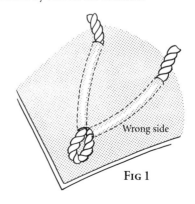

Wrong side

FIG 1

5 Make bias binding from your patterned fabric (see binding, page 25). Place the lining (which is the same fabric as the outer cover) on the wrong side of the quilting, and pin and tack the lower (straight) edges together. Bind the lower edges.

6 Take a spare piece of binding about 13cm (5in) long. Fold the edges to the middle, lengthways, then fold in half again to form a long strand with the raw edges enclosed. Machine stitch down the length. Now fold it in half to form a loop. Pin this on the right side of the quilted piece, in the middle and tack it into place (see Fig.2). Place both sides of the

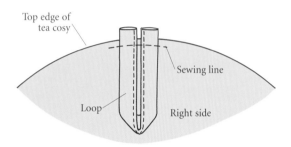

FIG 2

tea-cosy together with the quilting on the outside. Pin, tack and carefully bind the curved edge, making sure you have included all layers. Slipstitch the loop up onto the binding to finish.

POT HOLDER

With careful cutting, you should have enough fabric to make this handy pot holder as well as the tea-cosy.

Finished size: 25×23cm (10×9in)

1 Cut two pieces of patterned fabric 27×24cm (10½×9½in) and two pieces of wadding the same size. Sandwich the layers together and tack in place.

2 Machine quilt diagonal lines 5cm (2in) apart across the sandwich, then across the other way (see machine quilting, page 24).

3 Bind the pot holder, making a loop as you go in the same way as you did for the tea-cosy.

Detail of the knot pattern showing the raised effect of the Italian quilting

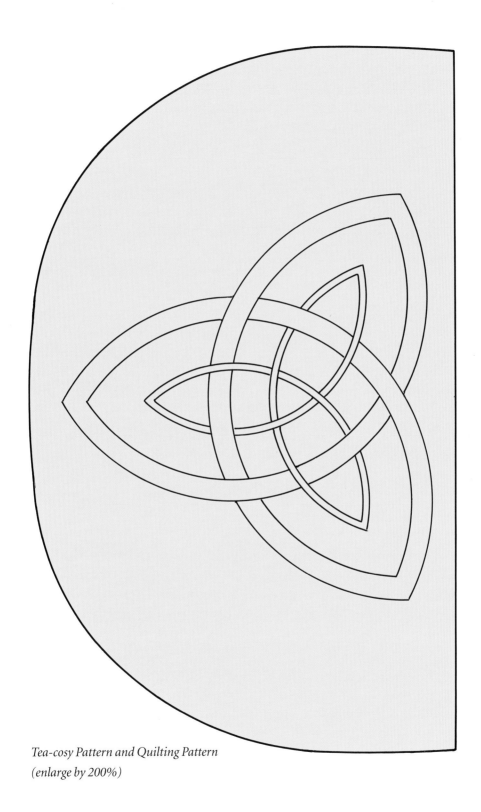

Tea-cosy Pattern and Quilting Pattern
(enlarge by 200%)

Under the Sea Cushion

This lovely cushion with its maritime theme uses the attractive technique of shadow quilting where the soft muted colour tones are achieved by using strong colour behind a sheer top layer, in this instance voile.

Finished size: 50cm (20in) square

YOU WILL NEED

Background fabric, 40cm (16in) square

Butter muslin, 40cm (16in) square

Sheer fabric, such as organza or fine voile, 40cm (16in) square

2oz polyester wadding, 40cm (16in) square

Selection of brightly patterned fabrics in pink, green and purple

Bondaweb, about 0.5m (½yd)

Toning fabric for the borders and cushion back, 0.75m (¾yd)

Threads to match the patterned fabrics

Three glass beads for fish eyes

Cushion pad, 46cm (18in)

1 Trace off templates A, B and C on page 79 and use to draw the outlines of three fish, four starfish and four shells onto the Bondaweb. Cut each piece out roughly, and iron them onto the patterned fabrics as follows.

Green: 1 fish, 2 starfish, 2 shells
Purple: 1 fish, 2 starfish, 2 shells
Red: 1 fish

Cut out all the pieces carefully.

2 Using the appliqué and quilting pattern on page 78 as a guide, lightly trace the whole design on to the well-pressed background fabric. Peel off the backing paper from the patterned fabric pieces and carefully place into position. Iron them into position following the Bondaweb directions.

3 Press the butter muslin and place on a flat surface. Place the wadding on top. Next lay on the background fabric, and finally the sheer fabric square. Make sure that the edges are matched up.

4 Tack all these four layers together in a grid pattern (see tacking up, page 21) then mount in a frame (see equipment, page 13) and quilt. Add an edging band (see page 10) down each side of the tacked fabric to make quilting in a frame easier. Whichever frame you use, clamp it to the border fabric, not the sheer fabric.

5 Using whichever coloured quilting thread is appropriate, carefully quilt around each of the appliqué pieces, including the fins and shell details (see quilting, page 21).

6 Trace off the seaweed design (template D) on page 79 and glue it to medium-weight card and cut out to make a template. Place the template onto the design and draw around it. Quilt along the drawn design. Finally sew the bead eyes onto the fishes.

7 Trim the design to 33cm (13in) square. Mark lines 10cm (4in) in from each edge of the quilted design and work a running stitch square for a decorative highlight.

8 Cut four pieces of border fabric 11.5×58.5cm (4½× 23in). Pin, tack and sew each side in place, taking care not to stitch into the seam allowance at the corners, and either butting or mitring the corners (see finishing corners, page 26).

9 The cushion back has an envelope opening for the insertion of the pad. To make this you will need to cut two pieces of the toning fabric, one measuring 48×54.5cm (19× 21½in) and one 26.5×54.5cm (10½× 21½in). Turn a small hem down the shorter edges of both pieces, then press open.

10 Lay the quilted piece wrong side down on a flat surface. Place the smaller cushion backing piece right side down on the quilting, matching the edges. Now place the larger piece on top, again matching the edges.

11 Taking a 0.5cm (¼in) seam allowance, pin, tack and sew the quilted piece to the backing pieces. Turn to the right side and press. Measure 5cm (2in) in from each edge of the cushion and sew a line of running stitches all the way around. To finish, insert the cushion pad.

Appliqué and Quilting Pattern

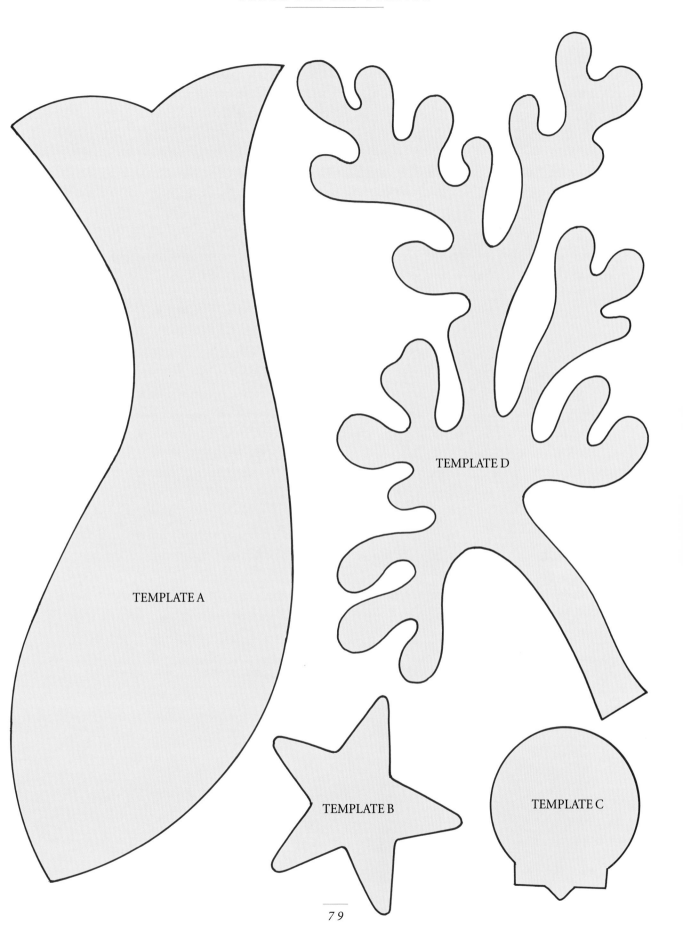

TEMPLATE A

TEMPLATE D

TEMPLATE B

TEMPLATE C

Devon Dumpling Cot Quilt

This soft baby's quilt is worked in motifs found in traditional West Country quilts. The name is often used for someone who hails from Devon, and since I am a dumpling in more ways than one, the name fits! It is worked on peach satin weave cotton, backed with the same fabric so it is reversible.

Finished size: 103×83cm (40½×32½in)

YOU WILL NEED

Satin weave furnishing fabric in the colour of your choice, 2m (2yd) by 122cm (48in) wide
2oz polyester wadding, 1m (1yd) by 127cm (50in)
Matching thread for quilting

1 First wash, dry and iron your fabrics. Cut the main fabric in half to make the front and back halves, then cut off the selvedge (the tightly woven edge) down one side. Cut four 4cm (1½in) wide strips for binding the quilt later. Press both pieces of fabric carefully.

2 The quilting pattern given is for one quarter of the quilt. Enlarge this to 330% on a photocopier then see page 16 for instructions on creating the full design. If the lines are faint, go over them with a felt-tip pen.

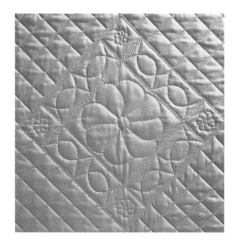

3 Mark the full quilting design on the shiny side of one piece of fabric.

4 Once the fabric is marked, the piece is prepared for quilting by first making a quilt sandwich (see tacking up, page 21). Using a quilting hoop (see equipment, page 13), quilt along all the marked lines with even stitches, as neatly as you can manage. As you get to the edge of the design, you will find you cannot fit it into the hoop or frame very easily so use an edging band (see page 10) to extend the borders to fit into the hoop.

5 If you wish, you can put a monogram of your initials in one corner and the year in another in place of the flowers shown.

6 Once all the quilting is finished, tack a line of stitches right around the quilt, approximately 0.5cm (¼in) away from the last line of stitching.

7 Remove the grid tacking, leaving the edge tacking in place. Measure 1cm (⅜in) from the last quilted line, and trim the three layers to this line.

8 Bind the quilt with straight strips made from the satin (see binding, page 25).

9 Make a label or embroider your name and the date of the quilt on the back.

Quilting Pattern (enlarge by 330%)

Country Scene Neck Purse

There can be few little girls around who don't like bags. Handbags, shopping bags, bum bags – any bags. Some however have to carry a bag and I designed this one for a very special girl – my Briony – who has to have her asthma inhalers with her at all times. We came up with endless ideas after this one – the country in winter and autumn, and the seaside. Perhaps she'll have a cupboard full one day. The bag can be hand or machine appliquéd.

Finished size (not including strap): 18×15cm (7×6in)

YOU WILL NEED

Blue fabric (for sky), 40.5×18cm (16×7in)

One packet of Stitch and Tear (see page 25)

Fabric for interlining, 39×17cm (15½×6½in)

Fabric for lining, 39×17cm (15½×6½in)

Scrap of striped fabric (for ploughed fields)

Scraps of green and white fabrics

Scraps of green fabrics (for trees)

2oz wadding, 39×18cm (15½×7in)

Matching bias binding, 1.75m (1¾yd) by 2.5cm (1in) wide

Animal buttons (I used three sheep and two cows)

Assorted matching threads for satin stitching and quilting

1 Enlarge the neck purse pattern on page 86 by 150% and cut one from the blue sky fabric and one from the Stitch and Tear. Mark the field placement notches on both edges of the blue sky fabric, then tack the Stitch and Tear to the back.

2 Enlarge templates A and B by 150% on a photocopier. Cut one template A in striped fabric and one template B in green fabric. Place piece B on to the right side of the purse pattern, matching the notches to the edges. Place template A on top of template B so they fit together. Pin and tack into place.

3 Satin stitch (see page 30) the edge of the green fabric into place, working to slightly under the striped fabric. Satin stitch the striped fabric into place along both raw edges.

4 Cut clouds in the white fabric using templates A and C from the Sweet Dreams Neck Pillow on page 96 *without* adding seam allowances and pin and tack them into place. Satin stitch around the clouds in white. Finally satin stitch the tree trunks in brown, where shown on the photograph.

5 Carefully sandwich the sky fabric, wadding and interlining together and tack (see tacking up, page 21) and choosing the appropriate colour thread, quilt around the hills and clouds (see quilting, page 21).

6 Bind along the straight edge of the neck purse (see binding, page 25). Take a 10cm (4in) length of bias binding, fold it in half and oversew along the raw edge. Fold in half to form a button loop. Pin and tack the button loop in the centre of the curved edge as indicated on the pattern to the wrong side with the raw edges together. Now bind along the curved edge, from 2.5cm (1in) below the straight edge to the same on the other side. Stretch the binding at the curves as you go to help it lay properly.

7 Fold the purse so the hills match front and back and secure with a pin. Then, starting at one edge, pin the remaining binding into place to 1cm (⅜in) past the binding edge. Place the other end at the corner of the other side and pin that to the same place. This will leave a long loop of binding to deal with later. Machine stitch the binding up the edges, fold it over and hem it down. Oversew the rest of the binding loop.

8 From the green fabric scraps, cut two 6.5cm (2½in) diameter circles and six 4cm (1⅝in) diameter circles. Using dark green thread, make eight yo-yos as described in the Pot of Gold Wall Hanging on page 46. Sew the yo-yos in place on the 'trunks', and sew on the sheep and cow buttons as indicated on the pattern.

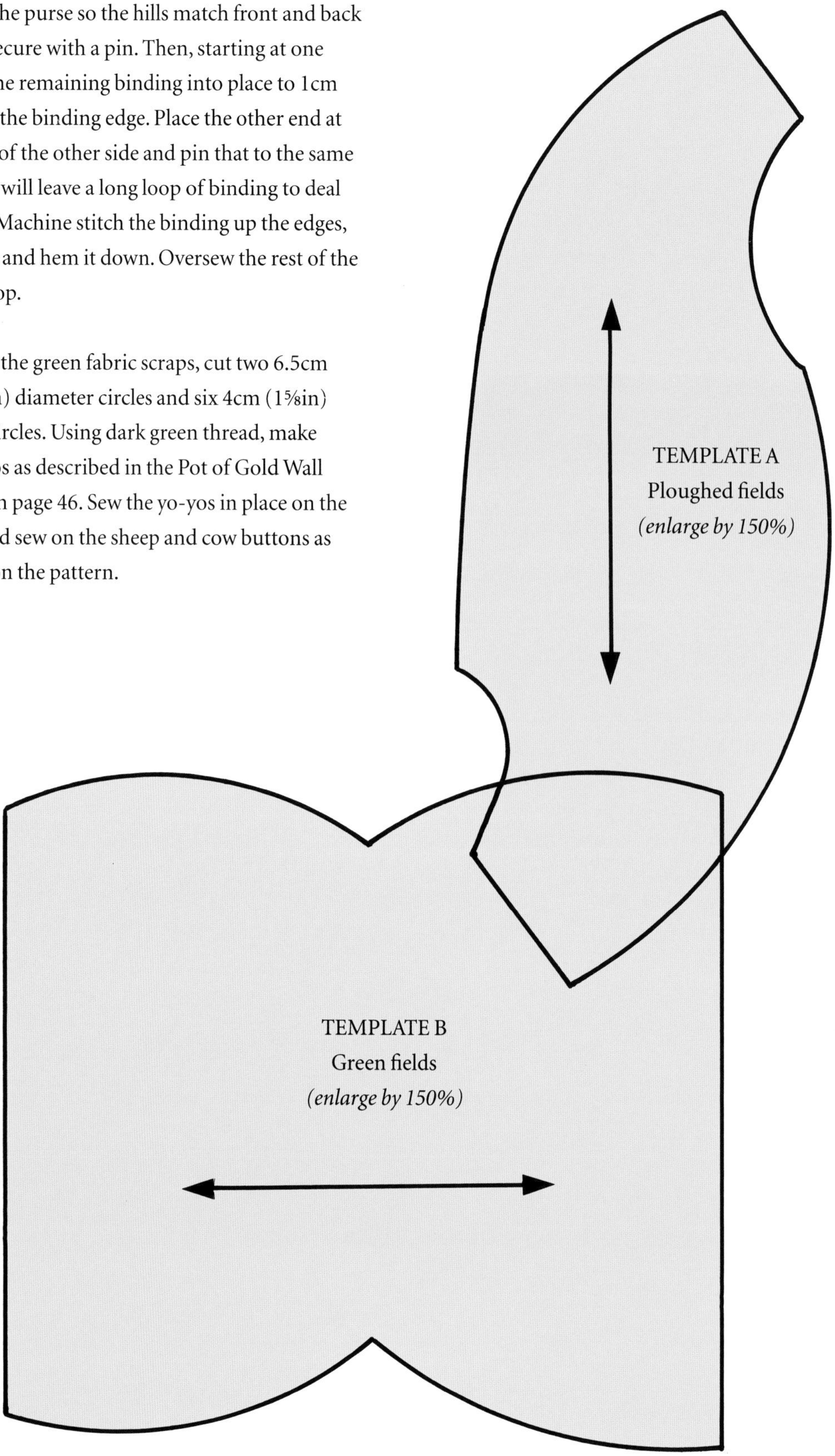

TEMPLATE A
Ploughed fields
(enlarge by 150%)

TEMPLATE B
Green fields
(enlarge by 150%)

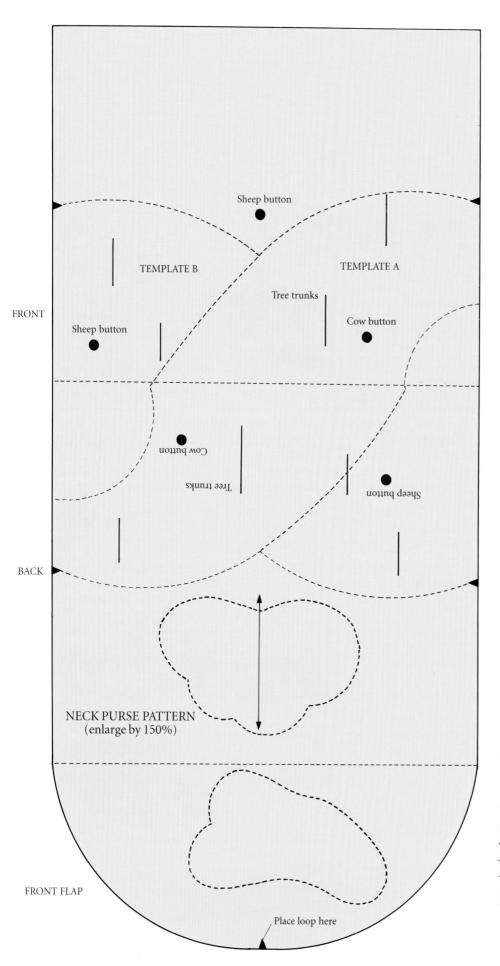

Sheep button

TEMPLATE B   TEMPLATE A

FRONT

Tree trunks

Sheep button   Cow button

Cow button

Tree trunks   Sheep button

BACK

NECK PURSE PATTERN
(enlarge by 150%)

FRONT FLAP

Place loop here

The Neck Purse Pattern shows the position of the appliqué templates, the tree trunks and the decorative cow and sheep buttons. Note that template B, the green fields, is positioned first, then template A, the ploughed fields, is placed on top taking care to match up the shaped edges.

Gingerbread Man Apron and Bag

This apron and bag set enables children to join in the fun of shopping and cooking. They are are washable and lined – the bag for extra stability and the apron for more absorbency. Buttonhole appliqué has been used, an efficient and decorative method of attaching one fabric to another, but I have also used fusible webbing to simplify the job and create a more durable finish.

Finished sizes: Apron 45×58.5cm (17¾×23in); Bag 24×25.5cm (9½×10in)

YOU WILL NEED

Outer fabric, 0.5m (½yd) by 112cm (44in) wide

Lining fabric, 0.5m (½yd) by 112cm (44in) wide

Scraps of fabric for appliqué

Scraps of Bondaweb (or other fusible webbing)

Medium-weight card

Bias binding in a contrasting colour, 4m (4yd) by 2.5cm (1in) wide

Embroidery thread (six strand) in toning colours

Matching sewing thread

Four round black beads

1 First wash, dry and iron your fabrics. Referring to Fig.2 (page 90), cut one apron piece (on the fold), one bag piece and two bag handles from the outer fabric. From the lining fabric cut one apron piece (on the fold) and one bag piece.

GINGERBREAD MAN APRON

To Make the Appliqué

2 From a fabric scrap cut the appliqué fabric background 20×13cm (8×5in). Put to one side.

3 Make a template for the gingerbread man (template A) with medium-weight card (see the box on page 91). Draw around the template on to the paper side of the Bondaweb. Cut it out roughly and iron onto the fabric for your man following the manufacturer's instructions. Cut out

along the drawn line, peel off the backing paper and place on the background fabric and iron into place. Buttonhole stitch (see page 29) around the man in toning thread.

4 Cut a 10cm (4in) diameter circle of white fabric for his hat. Tack around the outer edge with white thread, then gather up the stitches and fasten off. Pin this into place on the man's head.

5 Cut a piece of white fabric 6.5×3cm (2½×1¼in). Fold the two long sides to the middle, then turn 8mm (⁵⁄₁₆in) in from each end towards the middle. Pin this piece across the lower edge of the hat and buttonhole stitch in white around the edge of the hat.

6 Iron a piece of Bondaweb to the back of the white fabric. Following the apron outline on template A, cut an apron for the gingerbread man. (You may need to cut two pieces of fabric so the darker fabric doesn't show through.) Iron the apron into place and buttonhole stitch around it in white.

7 Using stem stitch (see page 30), sew the apron ties and the handle of the wooden spoon , as shown in the photograph. Embroider the bowl in satin stitch (see page 30). Sew black beads into place for eyes and then sew the mouth in straight stitch. Trim the appliqué backing piece cut earlier to 11.5×18cm (4½×7in).

To Make the Apron

8 Place the outer and lining pieces of fabric together and fold them in half. Measure 23cm (9in) down from the corner of the cut edges and mark it. Then measure 13cm (5in) from the corner towards the fold, and also from the 23cm (9in) mark. Make a mark here too. Place a tea plate on the fabric, mark and then cut a curve for the armholes. Use a dinner plate as a guide for the lower curve (see Fig.1).

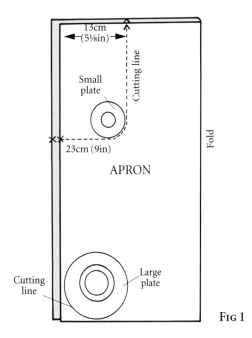

FIG 1

9 Pin the appliqué centrally on the bib of the outer fabric and buttonhole stitch into place. Then pin the outer and lining fabrics together. (Using safety pins at this point makes the future stages less painful to handle!)

10 Bind the top edge of the apron (see binding, page 25). With the wrong side of the apron facing, sew the binding along the lower curve of the apron from the first 23cm (9in) × mark to the second 23cm (9in) × mark. Turn to the right side, fold the binding and machine stitch into place.

11 Cut a length of bias binding 192cm (75½in) long. Measure 33cm (13in) and mark that

point with a pencil. Place this mark at the 23cm (9in) × mark (see Fig.1) on the wrong side of the apron. Taking a 1cm (⅜in) seam allowance, pin and machine stitch up to the ∧ 13cm (5in) mark. Leave 53cm (21in) of bias binding loose (this goes around the neck), then rejoin to the opposite ∧ 13cm (5in) mark. Stitch down to the 23cm (9in) × mark, then leave the end loose. Fold in 1cm (⅜in) at each end of the binding to neaten.

12 Turn to the right side of the apron and fold the binding in half. Pin and machine stitch the binding, continuing along the curved edge of the apron, then the loose length that forms the neck strap, down and along the second curve and, finally, along the other strap. Because you are sewing on the right side, make sure that your stitching is even.

When using this apron, place the neck strap over the head, put one tie through the neck strap from the back, then tie the two ties together. This will keep the bib from flapping forwards.

seam allowance, sew around the top, holding the two layers together. Pull the outer bag through the hole in the lining. Pin and sew the hole in the seam lining on the right side. Tuck the lining into the bag.

5 Fold 2cm (¾in) of each end of both handles back on itself, and pin into place, raw edge against the lining. Sew two parallel lines around the bag top, catching the handles in place as you do so.

GINGERBREAD MAN BAG

To Make the Appliqué

1 Make the appliqué panel in the same way as the apron, but place the umbrella pattern segments individually. Chain stitch (see page 29) over the joins and stem stitch the umbrella handle. Bind the appliqué panel with contrasting bias binding.

To Make the Bag

2 Fold both long edges of each handle into the middle, then fold in half lengthways, making four-layers with the raw edges enclosed. Machine a line of stitching 1cm (⅜in) from each edge to secure.

3 Fold the bag lining in half and taking a 1cm (⅜in) seam allowance, sew along the non-folded edge, leaving a 20cm (8in) space in the centre of the seam. Cut along the fold.

4 Taking a 1.5cm (⅝in) seam allowance, sew down the sides of both the inner and outer pieces. Turn the outer bag to the right side and place it into the lining, right sides together. Taking a 1.5cm (⅝in)

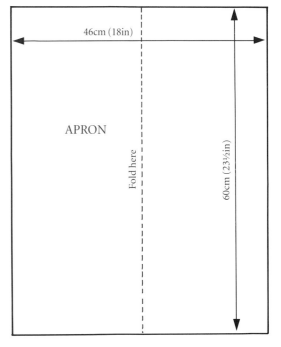

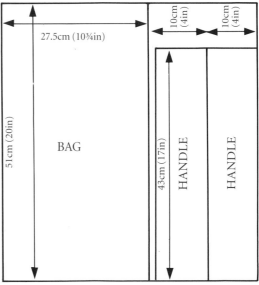

FIG 2

COMPOSITE TEMPLATES

The figures shown on page 91 and 92 are slightly different from those used so far in the book, in that they are composite templates, designed this way to show how the characters look when complete. The parts need to be made as individual templates – so for template A, the baker, the first template made is for the gingerbread man himself, that is only his head and body. The second template is for his apron alone. No template needs to be made for his hat as this is constructed from two pieces of fabric and described in steps 4 and 5.

Similarly, for template B, the gingerbread man template is made first, following only the outline of his body and head. The appliqué umbrella is then made, with separate templates for each segment of the umbrella.

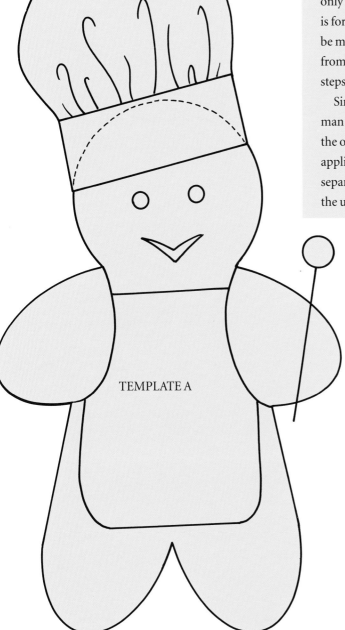

TEMPLATE A

TEMPLATE B

Sweet Dreams Neck Pillow

Neck pillows are amazingly useful for all sorts of occasions – you may use one when travelling as a car passenger for example, or keep one tucked between your large pillows to slip behind your head when reading in bed. They are surprisingly simple to make and cover, and would make ideal presents. You can fill them with hops or lavender to promote relaxing sleep, and make them as lacy or plain as you please. For this one, I have hand appliquéd simple cloud shapes with a sleepy message on them.

Finished size: 30×13cm (12×5in)

YOU WILL NEED

For the pillow:
White cotton fabric, 49×43cm (19¼×17in)
White thread
Small amount of polyester filling

For the cover:
Piece of fabric, 47×39cm (18½×15½in)
Scraps of white fabric
Lace, 98cm (38½in) long by 6cm (2⅜in) wide, cut in half lengthways
Blue embroidery silk for embroidered writing
Cord or ribbon for tying, two lengths 75cm (29in)

To Make the Pillow

1 First wash, dry and iron your fabrics. Fold the white cotton fabric in half lengthways and

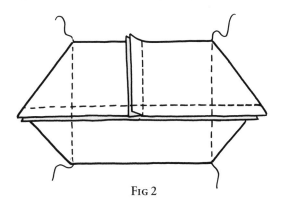

taking a 1cm (⅜in) seam allowance, sew the fabric into a tube (see Fig.1, seam A). With seam A in the middle, sew along the end of the tube, taking a 0.5cm (¼in) seam allowance (see Fig 1, seam B).

2 Now sew across the fabric at either end of seam B as shown in Fig.2. This will give neat, square corners to the pillow when turned through to the right side as illustrated in the photograph above.

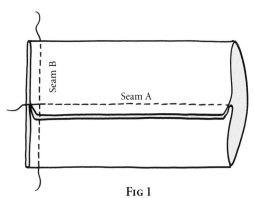

Seam B

Seam A

FIG 1

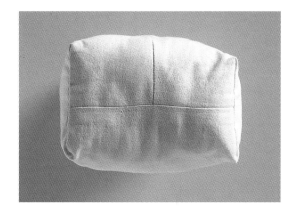

FIG 2

3 Now sew along the fabric at either end of the pillow, but leave an 8cm (3¼in) gap in the centre of the seam for stuffing. Again, at either end of the seam sew across the fabric to give good square corners.

4 Turn the fabric to the right side and, making sure the corners are sharp, stuff fairly lightly with filling – you don't want the pillow to be too hard. Oversew the opening closed. If you wish you could add dried lavender or hops to the stuffing at this stage.

To Make the Cover

5 Using the cloud templates A–D on page 96 make your appliqué clouds (see over papers appliqué, page 25). Using a coloured pencil write the messages on the right side of the fabric before tacking in the papers. Press the cover fabric and position the prepared appliqué pieces where you want them, being sure to leave space for the seams. Hemstitch the clouds into place.

6 Embroider suitable messages on the clouds in stem stitch (see page 30) using two strands of embroidery silk.

7 Fold the cover in half lengthways, right sides together, and, taking a 1cm (⅜in) seam

allowance, sew down the tube. Turn a 0.5cm (¼in) hem down at each end, and pin and tack one length of lace inside this hem, letting the ends of the lace overlap at the seam. Now machine stitch the lace and hem into place in one seam, then repeat 0.5cm (¼in) away (see Fig.3).

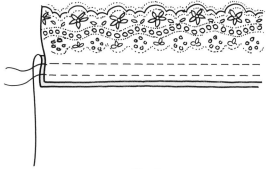

FIG 3

8 Taking one length of cord or ribbon, fold it in half and place the fold on the lengthways seam of the cover, 4cm (1½in) from the end of the fabric *not* the lace. Machine stitch the cord or ribbon into place by sewing over it several times. Repeat at the other end.

9 Slip the pillow inside the completed cover. To close up each end wrap the cord or ribbon around a couple of times before tying a bow. If using cord, place a knot near each end. If using ribbon, cut the ends into a point to help prevent unravelling.

TEMPLATE A

TEMPLATE B

TEMPLATE C

TEMPLATE D

Embroidery can be very effective when used to enhance patchwork, quilting and appliqué. It is probably best to limit the number of different stitches you use (see page 29 for some of the more common ones). The embroidery enhancement suggested for this project – a simple message in stem stitch – can be done in the hand, but for more complicated or extensive embroidery you may need an embroidery frame to keep your fabric taut. You may also wish to experiment with the type of yarn you use. There are so many wonderful types and shades available today – from the finest of silks to big, bold wool.

Stained Glass Appliqué Wall Hanging

This is a fabric interpretation of the lovely jewel-coloured decorative glass work seen in church windows. I have chosen a display of fruit for this small hanging which could fill a dark corner in a dining room or kitchen. This technique lends itself well to bright colours, since the dark leading makes the fabrics glow. Patterned fabrics can also be used for the coloured areas.

Finished size: 40×23cm (16×9in)

YOU WILL NEED

Background fabric, 0.5m (½yd)
Assortment of plain fabric scraps in bright colours
Two packs of thin, black bias binding
2oz wadding, 0.5m (½yd)
Backing fabric, 0.5m (½yd)
Black thread for appliqué and quilting
Small amount of brown embroidery silk

1 Enlarge the fruit pattern by 140% on a photocopier. Trace the complete fruit pattern lightly onto the background fabric. (Using a white pencil may help on a darker background.) Trace each coloured shape from the pattern, making sure not to reverse them. Pin the traced fruit shapes onto suitably coloured fabrics and cut out. Position each fabric fruit shape, excluding the cherries (see step 4) in the relevant place on the background fabric and tack all around to hold in place.

2 To create the leading effect, fold the bias binding in half lengthways prior to stitching it into place. Follow the fruit numbers on the design. Note where the lines start and finish and always end neatly under another line. Pin the strips of binding into place – lace pins might help here as they are shorter and the thread is less likely to catch on them.

3 Hemstitch (see page 29) the bias binding into place, taking care at the points of the leaves. For a leaf, stitch the bias binding down the middle first, then stitch the left line to the point of the leaf. Complete the right side next, ending neatly on top of the left line.

4 The cherries are treated differently from the other fruits because they are so small. First cut three cherries in black fabric, with a 0.5cm (¼in) seam allowance. Appliqué them into place, then appliqué three smaller red cherries on top of the black, giving the effect of an edging of bias binding.

5 After finishing the appliqué, stem stitch (see page 30) the stalks of the cherries and the pear with brown embroidery silk.

6 Sandwich the appliqué with the wadding and backing fabric (see tacking up, page 21). Quilt around and inside all the fruit and leaves, and quilt a random design on the background behind the appliqué (see quilting, page 21).

7 To finish, bind the whole piece with black bias binding (see binding, page 25) adding highlights and details with a fine, black, permanent pen if you wish.

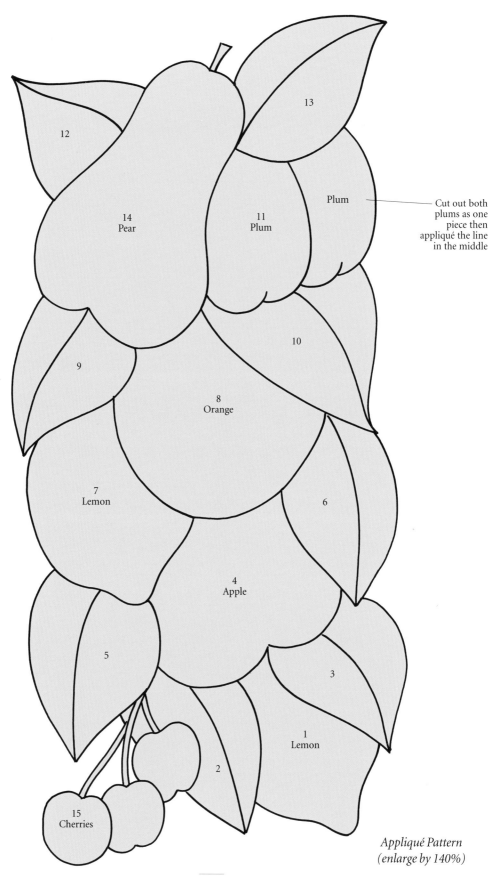

Cut out both
plums as one
piece then
appliqué the line
in the middle

Appliqué Pattern
(enlarge by 140%)

Southern Charm Lap Quilt

Stencilling is an ancient form of decoration which can be used on many surfaces. It is an excellent technique to combine with quilting, as quilting around the stencilled shapes avoids negotiating any seams! This quilt is stencilled with motifs reminiscent of the Native American Indian traditions of the United States. It is designed primarily as a lap quilt or car quilt.

The instructions given here are for this particular quilt and these stencils but you can easily create your own unique quilt by using whichever stencils you like and arranging them in your own way. There are hundreds of stencils available, from craft shops, DIY stores, mail order and even free with magazines.

Finished size: 145×110cm (57×43½in)

YOU WILL NEED

Plain sand-coloured fabric, 3m (3yd) by 112cm (44in) wide

2oz wadding, 1.5m (1½yd)

StenSource International Stencils (see Suppliers page 126) as follows:

  8in Lizard (P516);

  2in Broken Arrow Border (P546);

  4in Sun Medallion (P525);

  7in Sun Medallion (P520);

  3in Arapahoe Border (P537);

  Southwest Medallion (P515)

Masking tape

Fabric paints in turquoise, black, terracotta and yellow

Stencilling brushes

Matching quilting thread

Contrasting, checked binding fabric, 0.5m (½yd)

1 First wash, dry and iron your fabrics, then mark out the basic design following the quilting pattern given.

Stencilling (steps 2–4)
Stencil your designs only *after* practising on spare fabric or paper to minimise mistakes and save wastage of fabric. Once you are satisfied with your technique, you can proceed to stencil the designs one at a time.

2 Start by placing a stencil in the desired position on your marked fabric piece (it may be easier to hold it in place with masking tape).

3 Dampen your brush with water and dry it. Dip the tip into the paint and pick up a little dab. Work this into the brush by rubbing the tip on a saucer. Now brush away most of the paint onto scrap paper. When it seems so dry there can't be any paint left, the brush has the right amount of paint on it.

4 With the brush held upright, apply the paint onto the stencil with a stippling motion, pushing the bristles into the edges of the stencil to get a crisp edge. Repeat all over the stencil, then change to the next colour. It is best to use a separate brush for each colour. Go over the stencil with the second colour and so on *before* you are tempted to peep and peel off the stencil. Leave the stencilling to dry thoroughly, then press the fabric and use as required.

5 Using a light-coloured pencil follow the quilting pattern and mark your quilting lines on the stencilled fabric (see marking out a design, page 21). Some of the circular designs are smaller than others, so the quilting lines shown will be longer in places than others. Do not worry about this, it is only to provide an overall balance.

6 Tack or pin your three layers together to make a quilt sandwich (see tacking up, page 21). Quilt along all the marked lines (see quilting, page 21).

7 To finish, make the binding from the contrasting, checked fabric and bind your quilt (see binding, page 25).

Quilting Pattern

Ring Cushion

The tradition of a ring cushion at a wedding is a recent but rather charming one. The cushion can be made to match the bride's or bridesmaids' dresses, and perhaps be carried by a pageboy to give him something important to do. (The rings are tied with ribbon to the cushion to prevent disaster!) You can also add the names of the bride and groom and their wedding date for a lasting wedding souvenir. I have chosen a pattern of interlocking hearts in the tradition of Celtic work. The lines never end – like the love of the couple they represent.

Finished size (including frill): 23cm (9in) square

YOU WILL NEED

Plain, light fabric, three 15cm (6in) squares
Bridal fabric, two 20cm (8in) squares
Dark, contrasting (or flowered) fabric, 0.25m (¼yd)
Matching lace, 1m (1yd) by 2cm (¾in) wide
Ribbon to tone, 48cm (19in)
Matching thread
2oz wadding, two 16cm (6¼in) squares
Small amount of stuffing

1 First make the inner cushion pad from the two 15cm (6in) squares of plain, light fabric. Taking a 0.5cm (¼in) seam allowance, sew round all sides leaving a 4cm (1½in) gap in one edge for stuffing. Turn to the right side and stuff, pushing a knitting needle or swizzle stick into all the corners to make a neat pointed square. Set aside.

2 To make the cushion cover, start by making the bias strip for the appliqué. Cut bias strips 3cm (1¼in) wide in the dark contrast fabric. These strips do not need to be particularly long – 18cm (7in) each will do. Fold each strip in half lengthways and sew, taking a 0.5cm (¼in) seam allowance. Use a bias bar (see page 10) inserted into the channel formed to press the strip flat. Repeat with all the strips.

3 Press one square of your outer bridal fabric. Trace the interlocking hearts pattern (page 106) on to this using a light box or well-lit window (see marking out a design, page 21). Make a note of the under and over junctions on the appliqué as you must always stop and start under a cross-over seam.

4 Take a strip of bias, place one end on an under junction and pin into place. (It is best to use lace or sequin pins to anchor appliqué pieces into place as the thread is less likely to catch on short pins as you sew.) Sew along the inner edge of the bias strip taking small neat hemming stitches and removing the pins as you go. After 6cm (2⅜in) or so, go back and hem the outer edge. When you come to a point on a heart, sew right up to the next edge, then fold the strip back on itself to form a neat point, then hemstitch it into place as shown in Fig.1. Finish each strip at an under point and carry on until all the appliqué is complete.

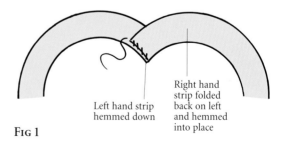

Left hand strip hemmed down

Right hand strip folded back on left and hemmed into place

FIG 1

The Service

5 Sandwich the finished appliqué square with two 16cm (6¼in) squares of wadding and one of the plain, light fabric (see tacking up, page 21). Quilt around the appliqué design, keeping close to the edge (see quilting, page 21).

6 Cut a strip of bridal fabric 9cm (3½in) wide by 94cm (37in) long (you can join strips if necessary). Join the ends of this strip to form a loop and then fold this loop in half lengthways and press, making the strip 4.5cm (1¾in) long.

7 Tack the lace to the raw edges of the loop, overlapping at the seam. Begin pinning the raw edges of the loop to the edges of the cushion, right sides together. Pleat the corners to take most of the bulk, though there can be two or three pleats along the edges too (see photograph). Once you have pinned, then tack and sew into place.

8 On the right side, topstitch close to the edge of the cushion top, catching the seam allowance for the frill in place so the frill stands out nicely.

Appliqué Pattern

9 Take a 20cm (8in) square of bridal fabric for the cushion back and press and tack a 0.5cm (¼in) hem down all round. Start to hemstitch it into place on the back of the cushion, inserting the inner cushion pad when you are three-quarters around. Be sure to place the edge of the pad under the seam allowance to create a smooth surface. The cover will be quite tight, but this is intentional as it gives a pleasing appearance.

10 Cut the ribbon in half and cut all the ends into points to help prevent fraying. Fold each ribbon into half again and pin at the points marked ∗ on the appliqué hearts pattern opposite. Sew securely into place with matching thread. Now that the ring cushion is completed all that remains to be done is to thread the rings onto the ribbons on the big day and to tie the ribbons securely into bows.

Detail of the Ring Cushion showing how the quilting enhances the interlocking hearts patterns

Cathedral Window Album Cover

This album cover can be tailored to fit any size album and makes a beautiful present for a newly wed couple. This version is made in pure silk, which is not really recommended for beginners as it is quite hard to handle. You can make a lovely example in patterned fabric as well as plain – how about using the bridesmaids' dress material with the bride's dress fabric in the centres? I have also added brass charms (see Suppliers page 126). These add a classic touch, though you could also include pearls or interesting buttons.

Finished size: 28×30.5cm (11×12in) (or depending on your album size)

YOU WILL NEED

A white or cream photograph album

Ivory silk (or print) fabric, 1m (1yd)

Scraps of coloured silk and brocade

Cream cotton fabric for lining, 0.5m (½yd)

Thin wadding, about 91cm (36in) long by 30cm (12in) wide

Threads to match

Brass charms and/or other embellishments

1 First make the Cathedral Window Square. Cut nine 17cm (6¾in) squares in ivory silk or patterned fabric. It may be easier to iron thin iron-on interfacing to the wrong side of the silk before cutting to help stabilise it. Spray starch ironed on to the wrong side will also help make the sewing easier as the fabric will be firmer and will hold a crease better.

2 Cut eight 4cm (1½in) insert squares of brocade fabric and four 4cm (1½in) insert squares of coloured silk.

3 Take one square of ivory silk and iron a 0.5cm (¼in) seam allowance to the wrong side on all

four sides. Repeat with the other eight squares. Fold the four corners into the middle and secure with a small stitch. Repeat with the other eight squares. Press thoroughly (once again, spray starch may help).

4 Fold the corners into the middle again and secure with two or three tiny backstitches. Repeat with the other eight blocks. Press thoroughly again.

5 Taking small stitches and with right sides together, oversew the nine blocks into a grid of three blocks by three blocks (see Fig.1).

FIG 1

6 Place a brocade insert over the junction of two blocks and pin into place (see Fig.2). Pull the edge of the folded silk square over and pin down, then slipstitch neatly into place (see Fig.3). Following the photograph on page 109, place the other inserts where you want them and oversew them into place on all four sides as described above.

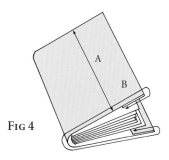

FIG 4

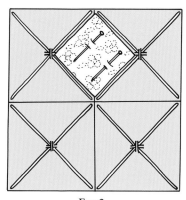

FIG 2

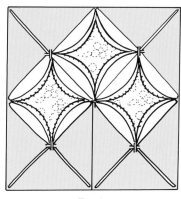

FIG 3

9 Place the layers as follows: wadding, silk and finally the backing fabric on top. Pin carefully and sew along a line on three sides, 0.5cm (½in) in from the edge. Trim the seam allowance to 3mm (⅛in) and turn through to the right side, pushing the corners out with a knitting needle. Press well, then machine zigzag or oversew the open end shut.

10 Wrap the cover around the album and tuck the flaps in. Pin one flap into place then neatly oversew it along both edges. Repeat with the other side.

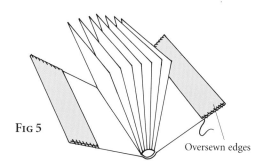

FIG 5

Oversewn edges

7 When the inserts are all in place and stitched down, turn the other fold edges down and slipstitch them. Add any embellishments you wish. Set aside.

8 Now make the album cover. Measure the album carefully (see Fig.4). Measurement A is the height of the cover and measurement B is the length of the two covers, the spine and two 13cm (5in) cover flaps. Mark these exact measurements onto the cotton lining fabric.

11 Slip the cover over the album board and slide into place. This will be very snug – it is meant to be. Simply stretch the fabric until it slides into place (Fig.5). Position the square of Cathedral Window on the front cover. Place it slightly higher than central, and when you are happy, pin the square into place, taking care not to let the pin scratch the album cover.

12 Slip the front cover off again and slipstitch the Cathedral Window square into place, then put the finished cover back on.

Double Wedding Ring Wall Hanging

This delightful design first became popular in the 1930s. The name reflects the design which looks like interlocking wedding rings. It is becoming a popular custom to give a quilt or wall hanging to newly weds to wish them a long and happy marriage. This four ring design makes a lovely wall hanging, but if you multiply the rings and therefore the fabric quantities needed, you could make a quilt!

Finished size: approximately 74cm (29in) square

YOU WILL NEED

Cream, 100% cotton fabric, 1.5m/yd by 112cm (44in) wide

Six patterned fabrics, 0.25m (¼yd) each (for arcs)

Two plain fabrics, 0.25cm (¼yd) each (for the corner squares)

2oz wadding, 81cm (32in) square

Bias binding purchased or home-made, 2m (2yd)

Pink quilting thread

This design is not one of the easiest, due to the curved seams. However, if you are very careful and follow the steps to the letter, there is no reason why you should be unsuccessful. Make sure you cut accurate templates, and match the notches on the curved pieces to help position them properly.

To Make a Practice Ring (steps 1 and 2)

Although time consuming, it is a good idea to make a practice ring, to check that the pieces fit together well. *Note:* The templates are given for hand piecing, therefore you must add 0.5cm (¼in) seam allowances. After you have made a practice ring do not automatically cut out all the pieces required for the full quilt. Adjust the ring if necessary, before wasting any fabric! Your practice ring becomes one of the four complete rings needed for the hanging.

1 Enlarge the templates given on page 115 by 133% on a photocopier. Cut the following fabric pieces (see rotary cutting, page 16).

Four C pieces in plain pink.

Four C pieces in plain blue.

Eight A pieces in patterned fabrics.

Eight AR, pieces (ie, piece A reversed) in patterned fabrics.

Thirty-two B pieces in four different patterned fabrics.

One D piece in cream.

Four E pieces in cream.

2 Following the diagrams shown on page 113, stitch the pieces cut out above for the practice ring by following steps 3–7 below. Mark your choice of fabrics by gluing a small piece of fabric on the relevant number in the piecing diagram Fig.1. This will help you get the piecing order correct.

To Make the Quilt

3 To proceed to making the actual quilt you will need to cut out the following fabric pieces.

Twelve C pieces in plain pink.

Twelve C pieces in plain blue.

Twenty-four A pieces in patterned fabrics.

Twenty-four AR pieces in patterned fabrics.

Ninety-six B pieces in four different patterned fabrics.

Four D pieces in cream.

Twelve E pieces in cream.

4 Piece the arcs first starting with an A piece. Place it right sides together with one B piece and sew along the marked line. Add the next B piece and so on until all the arc is complete, finishing with an AR piece. Make all the arcs in this way.

5 Place a small pencil mark on the seam at points marked 1 and 2 on Fig.1. Place one E piece right sides together with a completed arc. Matching the marks, pin them carefully together, then sew. Add the arc at the other side. Repeat with all the other arcs and E pieces.

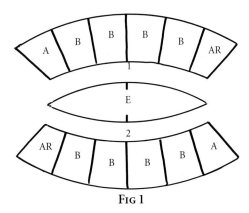

FIG 1

6 Add a blue C piece to each end of six of the arcs, and a pink C piece to each end of the other six. Again matching the marks, sew a completed arc set to each side of one D piece. Sew

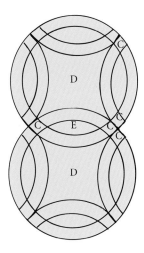

FIG 2

one completed arc set to three sides of another D piece. Sew these two pieces together, again matching marks (see Fig.2).

7 Sew an arc set to the top and bottom of a D piece, add another D piece to the bottom arc. Now add the final to arc sets to the top and bottom and right-hand side of the second D piece to complete the row. Pin and sew the rows together (see Fig.3).

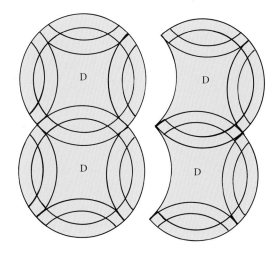

FIG 3

8 Press carefully with the seams away from the cream fabric, then using a silver pencil, trace the quilting pattern (page 114) onto the centre D pieces (see marking up a design, page 21).

9 Make a quilt sandwich (see tacking up, page 21). Then quilt the whole design (see quilting, page 21) and also quilt 3mm (⅛in) inside the pieced line on all D and E pieces.

10 Bind the wall hanging (see binding, page 25) and to finish, place a piece of fabric on the back with your name, the date and the names of the people you made it for and their wedding date if applicable – after all this is an heirloom!

Quilting Pattern

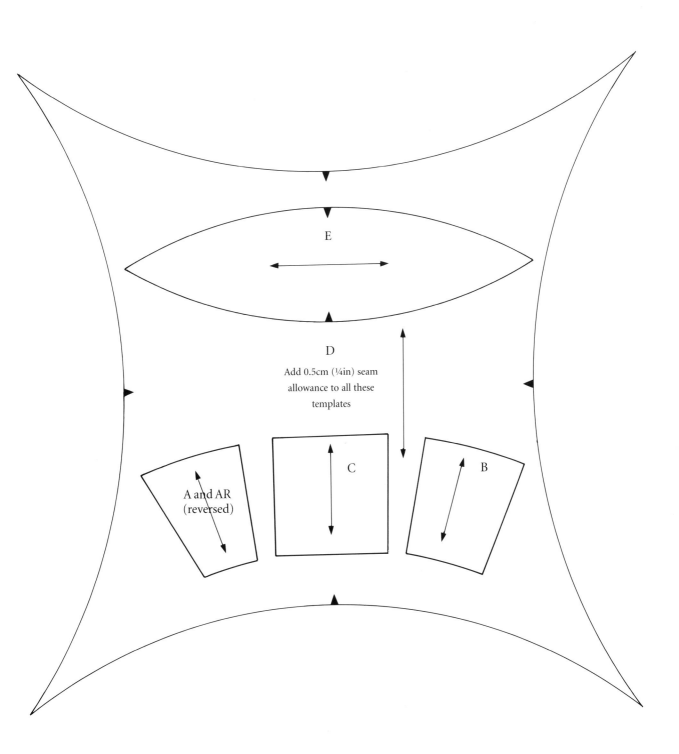

E

D

Add 0.5cm (¼in) seam
allowance to all these
templates

C

B

A and AR
(reversed)

Enlarge templates by 150%

Sashiko Tied Cushion

Sashiko is a Japanese quilting technique developed as a decorative way to hold layers of fabric together for warmth. Designs are often based on nature and are usually worked in thick white thread onto a dark blue background so the stitches are quite large. When used for decoration it is usual to sew two layers of fabric together without wadding. I have chosen a different colour for this wrapped cushion, which is loosely based on Japanese designs, but you can choose your own colour and size, and perhaps vary the patterns. Remember that the overall design should look pleasing when folded over the cushion.

Finished size: loose cover 60cm (24in) square; cushion 50cm (20in) square

YOU WILL NEED

Plain, light green 100% cotton fabric for cover, 0.5m (½yd)

Plain, dark green 100% cotton fabric for cover lining and cushion cover, 1.5m (1½yd)

Cushion pad, 50cm (20in) square

Three skeins embroidery silk to match darker fabric

1 Following the quilting pattern given on page 118 trace the design to be quilted onto the light green fabric (see marking out a design, page 21).

2 Cut four straight binding strips 1.5cm (⅝in) wide by 110cm (44in) long from the longer edge of the dark green fabric and set aside.

3 Place the light green marked fabric onto the dark green lining and pin or tack together. Using a larger needle than usual, such as a 'sharp' No.6, work with three strands of embroidery silk and quilt the design (see quilting, page 21). Start from the middle and work one section at a time. You may wish to practise your stitching on spare fabric first. Try to make stitches which are large, but just as even as those you normally aim for when quilting.

4 Make the inner cushion cover by first cutting two dark green fabric pieces 53cm (21in) square. With right sides together and taking a 1cm (⅜in) seam allowance, machine stitch around the square, leaving an opening to turn the cover through to the right side. Turn the cover, making sure the corners are sharp by pushing them out with a knitting needle or swizzle stick. Insert the cushion pad and slipstitch the opening closed.

5 Trim the outer cover so that it is even, then bind the edges as shown in Fig.1, leaving a long strand to oversew on each side (see binding, page 25). These now become the ties. To finish, place your cushion pad onto the outer cover and bring across two opposite ties and tie them into a bow. Pass the other two ties under this and tie another bow.

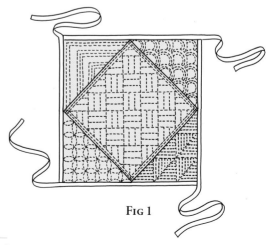

FIG 1

Quilting Pattern

Scrumpy Quilt

This quilt was initially inspired by the scrumptious apple fabric. It occurred to me that a series of quilts could be made using the same blocks in different colourways to reflect the seasons and this is my design for autumn. The basic quilt combines two blocks, Ninepatch and Snowball.

Finished size: 204×174cm (80×68.5in)

YOU WILL NEED

Four different fabrics in 100% cotton, all 112cm (44in) wide:

    apple fabric 2m (2yd);

    green fabric 0.75m (¾yd);

    mustard fabric 0.75m (¾yd) and

    dark red fabric 0.75m (¾yd)

Sheet of greaseproof or tracing paper

Backing fabric, 3.75m (4yd)

Wadding, single bed-size piece

Thread, dark red for quilting and green for sewing

Bought or home-made bias binding, 8.5m (8¾yd)

1 First wash, dry and iron your fabrics. Cut fifteen 32cm (12½in) squares of green fabric for the Snowball block. It would be useful if you made a template from card (see page 17).

Note: The seam allowance rule for hand or machine piecing is relevant here (see box on page 17).

2 Cut sixty triangular pieces in dark red fabric using template A on page 122.

3 Make pencil marks 10cm (4in) in from each corner on the right side of the each square as shown in Fig.1. Then make pencil marks on the wrong side of all the dark red triangular pieces, as shown on template A. Pin a red triangle to each corner of a green square, by matching up the pencil marks. Sew a line from mark to mark taking a 0.5cm (¼in) seam allowance (see Fig. 2, page 121). Continue to sew a red triangle to each corner of all the green squares in this way.

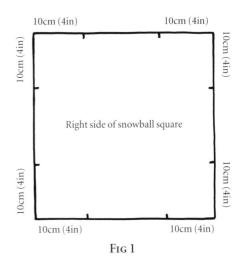

FIG 1

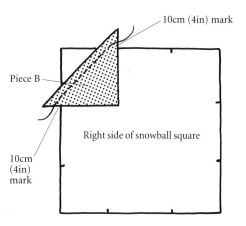

10cm (4in) mark

Piece B

Right side of snowball square

10cm
(4in)
mark

Fig 2

4 Using the apple fabric, cut two pieces 208×10cm (82×4in) and two pieces 180×10cm (71×4in) and put to one side for the borders. (It is important to cut the borders *before* smaller pieces to avoid having to join fabrics to make a border.)

5 Using template B cut fifteen squares in the apple fabric, sixty in the mustard fabric and sixty in the dark red fabric.

6 Using the piecing order shown in Fig.3 as a guide, join the Ninepatch blocks together by hand or machine (see hand piecing, page 17 or machine piecing, page 19). Press the blocks when joined (see pressing, page 18).

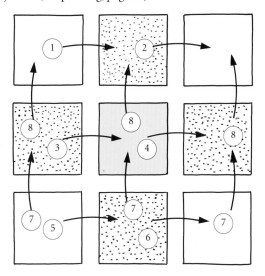

Fig 3

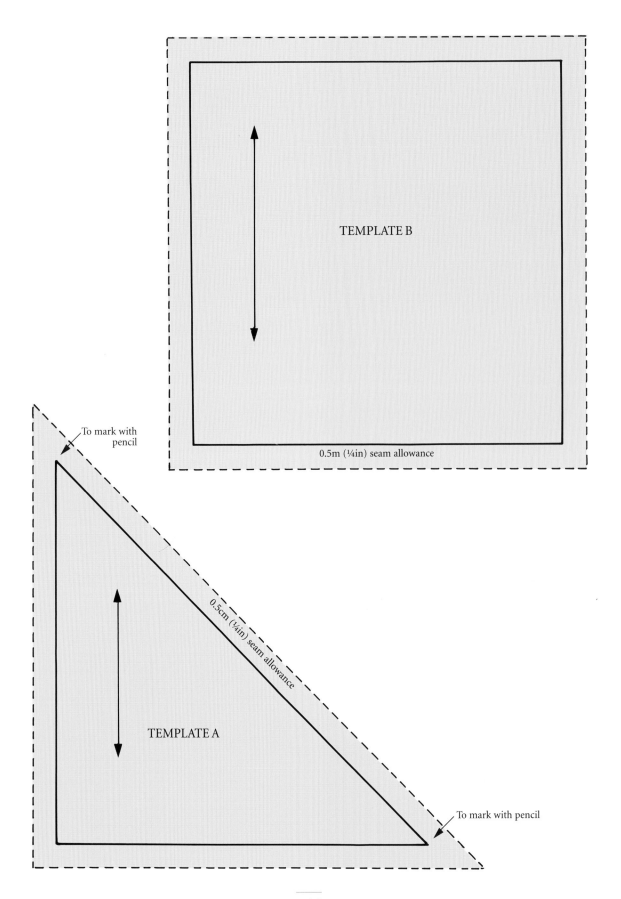

TEMPLATE B

0.5m (¼in) seam allowance

To mark with pencil

0.5cm (¼in) seam allowance

TEMPLATE A

To mark with pencil

Quilting Pattern

7 Trim the excess fabric from the Snowball blocks (see Fig.4) and press the red triangles back along the sewing lines as shown in the top right-hand corner of Fig.4. Join the Snowball and Ninepatch blocks as shown in the pattern on page 122, and press.

8 Fold one long apple fabric border piece in half and press. Measure 92.5cm (36½in) in from the fold each way and mark with a pencil dot. Repeat with the other long border piece. Using the fold and dots as markers, pin the border fabric evenly along each side of the quilt and then sew. Do not trim any excess.

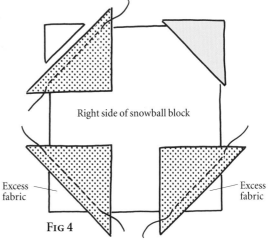

Right side of snowball block

Excess fabric

Excess fabric

FIG 4

9 Take the shorter apple fabric border pieces and fold each in half as for the long border pieces, but here the measurements should be 77cm (30¼in). Pin and sew as in step 8, mitring the corners as you go. Trim the excess fabric and press the top well.

10 Fold a 8cm (20in) square piece of greaseproof paper into quarters diagonally, open out and match the creases against the straight guide lines on Fig.5 (the two apple diagram). Match the central dot too and then trace the two apples. Turn the design through 45°, matching the lines and central dot again, and trace the next two apples.

Repeat twice more. You should now have a wreath of apples as in the quilting pattern on page 123. Using a light box or well-lit window, trace the design into the centre of each Snowball block, using your chosen marker (see marking out a design, page 21). Draw in the other quilting designs in the same way from the piecing and quilting pattern on page 125.

11 Make the quilt sandwich (see tacking up, page 21) and quilt the designs using dark red quilting thread (see quilting, page 21).

12 To finish, bind your quilt (see binding, page 25) and sign it.

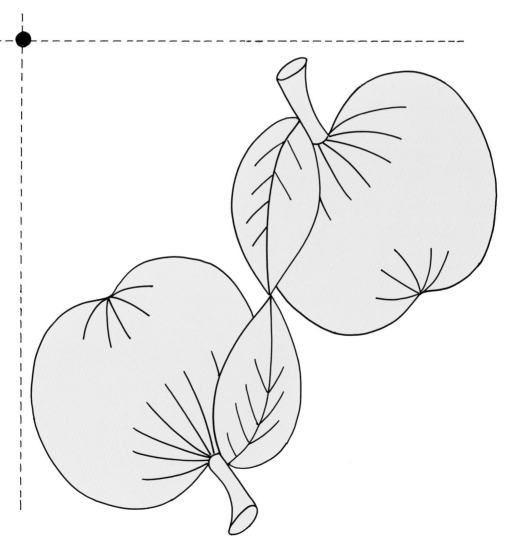

FIG 5

Piecing and Quilting Pattern

BIBLIOGRAPHY

The New Quilting and Patchwork Dictionary
GOLDBERG, RHODA OCHSER
(Crown Publishers New York , 1988)

The Perfect Patchwork Primer
GUTCHEON, BETH
(Penguin [out of print])

The Essential Quilter
CHAINEY, BARBARA
(David & Charles, 1993)

Through the Window and Beyond
EDWARDS, LYNNE
(That Patchwork Place, 1995)

The Complete Book of Patchwork, Quilting and Appliqué
SEWARD, LINDA
(Mitchell Beazley, revised 1996)

Yo Yos
MILLER, PRISCILLA
(American School of Needlework, 1994)

SUPPLIERS

A Pocketful of Charms
Ingsdon, 1 Highfield Close,
Malvern Link, Worcs WR14 1SH
Tel/Fax: 01684 893952
(Charms, miniature sewing kits, books, Alaska Dyeworks fabrics)

Quilt Basics
Unit 19, Chiltern House,
Waterside, Chesham,
Bucks HP5 1PS
Tel: 01494 791401
(Basic needlework equipment)

R&R Enterprises
13 Frederick Road, Malvern
Worcs WR14 1RS
Tel: 01684 563235
(Tubular quilting frames)

You Toucan Quilt
Windsor House, Greville Road,
Bedminster, Bristol BS3 1LL
Tel: 0117 9632599
(Fabrics)

Strawberry Fayre
Chagford, Devon TQ13 8EN
Tel: 01647 433250
(Fabrics)

Diane Dorward
27 Hawkwood Close, Malvern,
Worcs WR14 1QU
Tel: 01684 564056
(Stencils)

ASSOCIATIONS AND PUBLICATIONS

The Quilter's Guild
OP66, Dean Clough,
Halifax HX3 5AX

The National Patchwork
Association
PO Box 300, Hethersett,
Norwich, Norfolk NR9 3DB

Patchwork & Quilting Magazine
Traplet Publications Ltd., Traplet
House, Severn Drive, Upton-
upon-Severn, Worcs WR8 0JL

Popular Patchwork Magazine
Nexus Special Interests Ltd.,
Nexus House, Boundary Way,
Hemel Hempstead,
Herts HP2 7ST

Please note, there are many other mail order suppliers and shops – check in craft magazines for details.